THE PROTESTANT'S DILEMMA

D0594975

THE
PROTESTANT'S
DILEMMA

HOW THE REFORMATION'S

SHOCKING CONSEQUENCES

POINT TO THE TRUTH

OF CATHOLICISM

Devin Rose

SAN DIEGO
2014

The Protestant's Dilemma
How the Reformation's Shocking Consequences Point to the Truth of Catholicism
© 2014 by Devin Rose

All rights reserved. Except for quotations, no part of this book may be
reproduced or transmitted in any form or by any means, electronic or
mechanical, including photocopying, recording, uploading to the Internet, or
by any information storage and retrieval system, without written permission
from the publisher.

Unless otherwise noted, biblical citations are taken from the Revised Standard
Version of the Bible (© 1971 by Division of Christian Education of the National
Council of the Churches of Christ in the United States of America).

Published by Catholic Answers, Inc.
2020 Gillespie Way
El Cajon, California 92020
1-888-291-8000 orders
619-387-0042 fax
catholic.com
Printed in the United States of America

ISBNs
978-1-938983-61-0 print
978-1-938983-62-7 Kindle, electronic
978-1-938983-63-4 ePub, electronic

To my wife, Katie

CONTENTS

FOREWORD

Dialogue That Seeks Truth

Among the many profound teachings we have been blessed with from the Second Vatican Council, there is one that is particularly profound—though it was not really so much an individual teaching as a theme. That theme could be summed up by the word "dialogue."

The term was introduced in Pope Paul VI's 1964 encyclical, *Ecclesiam Suam*, and from there the term found its way into the documents of Vatican II and into the very life of the Church.

By "dialogue," our Holy Father, and the Council, did not mean to reduce the Catholic Church to the level of "one voice among many equals" with regard to the possession of truth. *Lumen Gentium* 14 declared:

> This Sacred Council... teaches that the Church, now sojourning on earth as an exile, is necessary for salvation. Christ, present to us in His Body, which is the Church, is the one Mediator and the unique way of salvation. In explicit terms He Himself affirmed the necessity of faith and baptism and thereby affirmed also the necessity of the Church, for through baptism as through a door men enter the Church. Whosoever, therefore, knowing that the Catholic Church was made necessary by Christ, would refuse to enter or to remain in it, could not be saved.

"Dialogue" is a dynamic term calling all of us as Catholics to enter into a real back-and-forth with all of humanity, grounded in Jesus Christ as God's "dialogue" with the world in the Incarnation. In Christ, God reveals the truth of who he is and who we are, but he also invites a response... a *dialogue*.

Liturgically, we Catholics understand this notion of dialogue well, even if not by that appellation. In the liturgy, God both speaks to us and we speak back to God. And we do not do so as mere puppets on a heavenly string. The many rites and churches within our Catholic communion speak back to God in many different languages and with differing nuances while never diminishing in the least the essential truths of the Faith—our Catholic identity.

The Council fathers, following Pope Paul VI's lead, invited us to expand our understanding of dialogue. and to invite the entire world into that dialogue as Christ's ambassadors. That means first to engage our own members in full communion with the Catholic Church. But it does not stop there, any more than Christ's communication of himself ceases at the doors of our churches. It continues in our relationships with our separated brethren who do not enjoy full communion with the Church, with those of non-Christian sects, and even with those who have no faith at all.

In this book, Devin Rose makes a valuable contribution to that dialogue, and specifically to our continuing dialogue with members of the thousands of Protestant sects. He also brings to the fore what can happen when we engage in the dialogue well. So many Catholics do not heed the Council's call because we just don't know how to do it. We don't know what to say. Devin Rose lays out for us a game plan. His book is structured as talking points that help us to be able to lead a Protestant in a dialogue to consider what he probably has never considered before. He leads the Protestant to see the untenable conclusions that necessarily follow from the theology he has, very often anyway, taken for granted.

From the four marks of the Church, *sola scriptura*, and the issue of authority, to baptism, marriage and much, much more, *The Protestant's Dilemma* presents both the Protestant position, pulling no punches in revealing the manifold theological holes in Protestant theology, and the Catholic position that alone can fill in those holes. The success of the text lies in the back-and-forth—*in the dialogue*. But it is not dialogue for dialogue's sake. It is dialogue with an end in mind of bringing all involved in the dialogue to the fullness of truth that the Catholic Church *alone* possesses in fullness.

That is what authentic *dialogue* in the conciliar sense is all about.

INTRODUCTION

Protestant Premises and the Road to Rome

I had been a baptized Christian for only a few months, after growing up "unchurched" and then giving my life to Jesus during my senior year in college, when I began to grow uneasy about why we Christians were so divided from each other. The Southern Baptist beliefs I espoused were different, on matters both big and small, from those of other denominations, and we certainly didn't worship with them. They had their church, and we had ours.

So began my period of inquiry about the lack of Christian unity and whether it was a problem. How had I, a newly minted Christian, come so quickly to a conclusion about which denomination taught the real truth?

I realized then that all I had learned about Christianity came from an Evangelical Protestant perspective. My friends had bought me a large, well-annotated New International Version of the Bible; I read it from cover to cover and then read it again. When I didn't understand something, which was often, I would look down to see if there was an explanatory note about it, and I usually found one—given through an Evangelical Protestant filter. When I had questions about Christianity, I would ask my Evangelical friends, and they would answer me according to what they believed was true. Meanwhile I prayed that Jesus would guide me into the denomination that was truest. Having discovered him, I wanted to be as close to him as possible.

I assumed that the Bible had to be the sure basis for truth, because I believed it was the inerrant word of God. That sounded pretty good, but two problems occurred to me: First, other Protestant denominations claimed the same thing, and yet we were divided from them in our beliefs; and secondly, the Catholic Church claimed there were seven more books, not included in our Bible, that were also inspired by God.

The first problem, it seemed to me, forced us to conclude that it was possible for different Christians—all claiming to be "led by the Holy Spirit" and all basing their beliefs on "the Bible alone"—to veer off in different, mutually exclusive directions. Throughout history, I discovered, some person or group within a Protestant church came to believe differently than the others and broke off to form his own, new denomination. Since the Holy Spirit is the Spirit of Truth and would never lead people to believe something untrue, at least some of the Christians who thought they were listening accurately to the Spirit's promptings, in reality were not.

The second problem was of a different sort, because it struck at the root of my faith: We believed in the "Bible alone," which meant we had to know with confidence which books made up the Bible. Yet here we had the Catholic Church claiming that my Bible was missing seven books that God had inspired and therefore desired to be included. How did I know who was right?

I finally concluded that one of two things must be true: Either the Holy Spirit had *tried* to guide Christians to know which books belonged in the Bible and we still got some of the books wrong; or the Holy Spirit succeeded, making sure the Bible was made up of the exact books that God himself inspired.

In other words, God either preserved his Church throughout history from errors that would corrupt its teachings, or he did not, in which case we could only be *somewhat* confident that *most* of our beliefs were *hopefully* true.

Hoping that the former was true, I wondered: Which denominations had the boldness to claim that they were that Church that held the fullness of the truth? (My Baptist church certainly didn't claim that.) It turned out that Catholics, Orthodox, and Mormons did. Of these, only Catholics and Orthodox had credible historical and theological claims—but both were a long way from my Evangelical Protestantism.

I was dumbfounded and unsettled. The Catholic Church taught things about Mary, purgatory, the saints, the sacraments, and priests that I thought were completely bogus. But I tried to set this bias aside and be objective. With a sense of dread, I began investigating the Catholic Church in earnest, looking and hoping for something that would let me off the hook to return to Protestantism in peace.

Alas, I failed to find it.

I challenged my Evangelical friends to prove my arguments wrong and explain where I was going off course. They tried to do so, but could not explain, for example, why I should accept the Protestant canon of Scripture—or *any* canon, for that matter. I studied books, took part in Internet discussions, and read stories of faithful and intelligent Protestants converting to the Catholic Faith. Finally I was received into the Catholic Church at Easter, 2001. Two of my Evangelical friends came to the four-hour-long vigil Mass. (I greatly respect and love all my Protestant friends; I would not be the new man that I am today without them.)

My road to Rome began with taking the risk that God might be real, with the discovery that he loved me and was worth trusting. As I trusted him, I felt confident enough to question myself—including my Protestant perspective.

It was never a question in my mind that God is a reasonable being. I assumed it to be true, because even as an atheist

I observed that the world functioned in a logical manner: Scientific laws were provable, mathematics could produce correct answers to problems, and deductive and inductive reasoning were demonstrably useful for understanding reality. The Christian faith, therefore, must also be supported by sound reasons, even if its truths also exceeded the limits of what reason could prove.

I brought such an analysis with me into my newfound faith, and I discovered that Protestantism's tenets led to untenable conclusions. It simply was not possible to maintain a reasonable basis for my Christian faith while remaining Protestant. At least one *ad hoc* leap was required—accepting a given set of books as inspired Scripture—but once I chose to endorse such a leap, I had no basis to criticize someone who made a different leap (say, for instance, that the Book of Mormon or the Koran was also inspired by God).

Twelve years later, I've had a lot of time to reflect on these and other Protestant premises and how they result in logical absurdities. (It's not that Protestants are absurd—far from it—but at the foundation of their beliefs is a hole that, for most, remains unexamined.) As time passed, I collected these premises, and the absurdities they led to, and put them together into this book.

Each section begins with a hypothetical statement, that if some premise of Protestantism were true, something else should logically follow. I then provide evidence that supports my claim that Protestantism does indeed accept the premise, and that the resulting logical conclusion is inevitable. Because Catholicism is true, the conclusion forced by the Protestant premise is absurd, and in each section I explain why that is so, giving the evidence (historical, theological, and rational) that supports the Catholic position. I conclude each section with a brief recap of the absurdity that Protestantism forces one to accept.

My ultimate goal, of course, is to demonstrate that the Catholic Faith is more plausible than Protestantism; that the Catholic Church is what it claims to be. In so doing I hope to clear away obstacles to believing in everything that Christ's Church teaches and proclaims to be revealed by God.

But what do I mean by *Protestantism*? Many Christians object to being classified as Protestants, because the term signifies a protest or *rejection* of something—namely the Catholic Church—rather than something positive. I understand this; however, we are often stuck with the semantics that history has produced, and Protestantism is the broad name given to the movements (and their descendants) that broke from the Catholic Church in the sixteenth century.

Therefore in this book I have chosen to use the term as it has been historically used, which means that Anglicans, Anabaptists, Lutherans, Calvinists, Evangelicals, and non-denominationals are all Protestant. They are not Catholic, or Orthodox, or Coptic. They all trace their origin to the 1500s and they all believe in the core principles of the Reformation: *sola scriptura* and *sola fide*, the sixty-six book canon of Scripture, the rejection of apostolic succession, and so on. Even though there are many differences among Protestants, and even though some point in this book will more closely apply to, say, Calvinists over Methodists or Pentecostals, these common beliefs enable us to speak and to reason about Protestantism as a whole.

————

Arguments alone cannot a Catholic make; faith is required, and God is ready to give it. But the assent of faith is usually not a blind jump that hopes to land on solid ground by happenstance. Rather, it is supported by motives of credibility.

I can only plod along with you to help you reach that

point of decision. From there, it is up to you to accept the wings the Holy Spirit gives you so that you can launch and fly. So put on your thinking cap, say a prayer, and join me in this exploration of our Christian faith: the history, the people, the theology. Let's see what we discover!

THE PROTESTANT'S DILEMMA

PART I

THE CHURCH OF CHRIST

1

DIVINE AUTHORITY

IF PROTESTANTISM IS TRUE,

Christ revoked the authority that he gave to the Church when he founded it.

We know that Christ established a Church, visible and unified, to which he gave his divine authority. In Matthew's Gospel we read that "he called to him his twelve apostles and gave them authority over unclean spirits, to cast them out, and to heal every disease and every infirmity" (Matt. 10:1). But according to Protestantism, this authority must have been lost when that visible Church became morally and doctrinally corrupt.

The Fall of the Church

The vast majority of Protestants believe that the visible Church did in fact *lose* God's authority at some point in time; that Christ *revoked* it when *corruption* entered into its teachings. Many fundamentalist Protestants believe that the date when the Church became corrupted and lost God's divine authorization was the year 313, when Constantine proclaimed the Edict of Milan, which ended the persecution of Christians in the Roman Empire and began (they say) the mixture of pagan corruption with the true gospel.

But Protestants in general are usually not so exact in their dating estimates, and instead claim that corruption entered into the Church somewhere between the second and sixth centuries. The dates vary according to when a particular Protestant, in studying the historical evidence, discovers a doctrine or practice of the Church that he believes is heretical. John Calvin describes the pervasive nature of the Church's corruption:

> The light of divine truth had been extinguished, the word of God buried, the virtue of Christ left in profound oblivion, and the pastoral office subverted. Meanwhile, impiety so stalked abroad, that almost no doctrine of religion was pure from admixture, no ceremony free from error, no part, however minute, of divine worship untarnished by superstition.[1]

The notion that "the Church" became corrupt nonetheless does not sit well with Protestants, since they also believe the Bible passages that speak in exalted terms about the Church. Their solution is to separate the historical institution originally known as "the Church"—which fell into corruption— from the true Church of Christ, which continued undefiled. At the time of its corruption, whenever that was, the visible institution became the Roman Catholic Church, while Christ's true Church became invisible and purely spiritual. Hence, the promises Christ made in the Bible still apply to all "true believers" in the world, who make up this invisible Church: the one that quietly endured through all the apostate centuries until the Reformation unearthed it.

No matter the particular date given for the corruption, it is common Protestant wisdom that by the fifteenth century, the Catholic Church had devolved into such a disaster of human traditions and theological errors that the only solution was a clean break: to make clear the difference between the true Church of the Bible and the corrupted impostor.

BECAUSE CATHOLICISM IS TRUE,

The Church has never lost the divine authority that Christ gave it, and corruption has never polluted its teachings.

In Luke's Gospel, Jesus says to his disciples: "Whoever listens to you listens to me. Whoever rejects you rejects me. And whoever rejects me rejects the one who sent me" (10:16). Notice the direct line of authority: The Father sends the Son, and the Son sends the apostles with his authority, such that listening to them (and the men whom they in turn authorize) is equivalent to listening to Jesus and the Father. We see how closely Christ associates himself with his Church when he knocks Saul (who later becomes Paul) off his horse:

> Now Saul, still breathing murderous threats against the disciples of the Lord, went to the high priest and asked him for letters to the synagogues in Damascus, that, if he should find any men or women who belonged to the Way, he might bring them back to Jerusalem in chains. On his journey, as he was nearing Damascus, a light from the sky suddenly flashed around him. He fell to the ground and heard a voice saying to him, "Saul, Saul, why are you persecuting me?" He said, "Who are you, sir?" The reply came, "I am Jesus, whom you are persecuting" (Acts 9:1–5).

Notice that Jesus didn't say, "Saul, why are you persecuting *my followers,*" but rather, "Why are you persecuting *me*?" For in murdering the leaders of Christ's Church, Saul was rejecting not only them but Christ himself.

From history, we see the apostles and then their successors, the bishops, exercising this authority in the Church, and the Church thriving under their divinely authorized leadership—even in the midst of horrific persecutions. From the Bible and early Christian writings, we understand that the authority Christ gave to the apostles as the leaders of his Church was transmitted to their successors. Paul speaks of this authority in his first letter to his disciple, Timothy: "[D]o not neglect the gift that is in you, which was given to you through prophecy with the laying on of hands by the council of elders" (1 Tim. 4:14). In the next chapter, he enjoins Timothy to "not be hasty in the laying on of hands" to avoid ordaining an unworthy man to lead the church (1 Tim. 5:22). Clement of Rome and Ignatius of Antioch, in the late first and early second centuries, testify to the authority given bishops as successors to the apostles.

Likewise, in order to make sense, the promises that Christ made to the Church must be understood as permanent; nowhere does Jesus say that at some point he would abandon his Church to let the gates of hell prevail against it (indeed he says the opposite) or that the authority he had given its leaders would be revoked.

The claim that the Emperor Constantine founded the (corrupted, visible) Catholic Church is an old myth with no evidence to recommend it. The Edict of Milan did not make Christianity the state religion of the empire; it merely provided for official toleration of Christianity within Roman borders, so that Christians could worship God without being persecuted for it. It's true that Constantine ceremonially opened the first ecumenical council of Nicaea in 325, but he did so as a temporal leader concerned with political stability, since the Arian heretics had caused such conflict in his realm. In any event, the council he summoned confirmed Christ's true divinity and produced the first part of the Nicene Creed (both of which Protestants accept)—hardly something a corrupt and heretical Church would do.

Since most Protestants do not give a specific event and date for how and when corruption entered the Church but instead mention a vague span of centuries, it is best to consider the plausibility of the assertion in general. Interestingly, it differs from the theology of the Mormons (Latter-Day Saints) only in the date given, for Mormons believe that the Church lost the authority Christ gave it sometime around A.D. 70 or 100 (either at the death of Peter or of the last apostle). At that time, they assert, the "Great Apostasy" began, which lasted for around 1,700 years before Christ *reestablished* his authority in the Mormon Church through Joseph Smith.

Does the Mormon claim seem plausible? The Word became flesh, pouring his life and wisdom into his disciples, inaugurating the era of the Church, the New People of God. Then, Christ gave us the Holy Spirit, the spirit "of power, of love, and of self-control" (2 Tim. 1:7), whom he promised would lead the apostles (and thus the Church) into all truth (see John 16:13). But the Mormon assertion means that the Holy Spirit *utterly failed* to lead the Church into all truth. Indeed, as soon as the last apostle died, the Church went belly-up for longer than 1,700 years! The gates of hell indeed prevailed against the Church, necessitating its reestablishment through a new revelation. Christ failed to keep his Church together and protected from adulterated teachings for even *one generation* beyond his life on Earth.

This key claim of Mormonism is not credible, even to most Protestants, yet the Protestant corollary is substantially similar, differing only in the number of years it took for corruption to taint the Church and its teachings and in the manner of the "true" Church's re-constitution.

Even as a Baptist, I rejected the Mormon claim of the Church losing its authority at the death of the apostles, but as I pondered this question, I had to admit that my Protestant beliefs *were not so very different.* When did *I*, as a Baptist, think that corruption had entered into the Church's teachings? The truth was that I had never given it much thought. "It happened in the first four or five centuries perhaps," I mused vaguely. And, like most Protestants, I thought that the Reformers had more or less corrected the corrupted teachings and set things right again. What did I think had happened to the Church for the thousand years between the corruption and the Reformation? To be honest, I didn't really think about it—nor do most Protestants.

Since Christ established a visible Church in the first century and gave it rightful authority, the burden of proof falls on Protestants to demonstrate that he revoked this authority universally from the Church at some point in time. What event can they point to that caused Christ to take away his authority, and which Church leaders were involved in it? Where is the historical evidence for the claim? I have asked this question to many knowledgeable Protestant apologists and pastors and have yet to receive a definite answer. The fact is, no event or even century can be pinpointed that can carry the weight of such a momentous claim, so the fallback is the idea that false teachings crept slowly into the Church and eventually tainted the gospel beyond recognition.

There is another problem with the Protestant version of events. Realizing the problematic nature of asserting that Christ's Church became corrupted, most Protestants will fall back to the claim that the *true* Church remained pure but was simply invisible. We know from history, however, that Christ founded a visible Church, and the members of his Church were unified together as his mystical Body, of which he is the head.[2] A body is both visible and alive; if you found a severed hand, a foot, an arm, and a toe on the ground, you would not say, "Here is a body," but rather, "Here are parts that were severed from a body."

Similarly, the Church is a visible unity that can be seen acting in history, with Christ's authority, to exclude from the Mystical Body those members who persisted in teaching false doctrines. Vincent of Lerins demonstrated the visibility of the Church when he wrote in the year 434:

> What then will a Catholic Christian do if a small portion of the Church has cut itself off from the communion of the universal faith? What, surely, but prefer the soundness of the whole body to the unsoundness of a pestilent and corrupt member.[3]

If the true Church is invisible, it becomes impossible to determine who has authority to excommunicate another. Christ directed the apostles on how and when to excommunicate someone from the Church (see Matt. 18:17), but what does this mean when the Church is invisible and spread out across numerous denominations? A Christian "excommunicated" from one church just goes to another down the street, both a part of the "invisible Church," rendering these biblical passages meaningless. Being excommunicated from the Church makes sense only if the Church is a visible unity that one can be cut off from.

THE PROTESTANT'S DILEMMA

If Protestantism is true, then either Christ revoked the authority he had given his Church or the Church changed in its essentials from being a unified, visible, and hierarchically organized body to an invisible and purely spiritual association. There is no scriptural evidence for the former and much against it, and in the latter case it becomes impossible to know to whom God has given the rightful authority to lead the Church. Protestants may like to speak of "the Church," but in truth all they can point to are individual believers who may or may not meet in some local congregation.

2

THE PAPACY

IF PROTESTANTISM IS TRUE,

After centuries of its existence, God decided to eradicate the office of the papacy.

The Church had a pope, a visible head, from the beginning. In fact, we know the names and approximate dates of all of the popes, all the way back to the first century: Peter first, then Linus, Anacletus, and Clement I. But sometime between the first centuries of the Church and the Protestant Reformation in the 1500s, the papacy as an office must have become corrupted, and God revoked his authority from it.

No Pope Needed, Thank You Very Much

Protestants diverge on myriad doctrines, but on one issue they stand fully unified: They reject the notion that the pope has any authority from God. They don't need a pope; they don't want a pope, and, they say, neither does God.

The pope is not needed because Protestants have the Bible. They would rather trust in an unchanging written document than the vicissitudes and caprice of human personalities. For them it seems more plausible that God would ordain such a standard. As one commenter put it to me:

Man cannot be trusted; man will corrupt what he touches. The survival of the scriptures is the survival of a touchstone to the apostles that serve[s] as an unchanging standard. This is a necessity; this is preservation; this is God's will.[4]

The pope is a mere man and thus fallible. God wouldn't have relied on a string of such men to lead his Church. Instead, he providentially had the apostles record divine truth in the Bible, where all Christians could find it and know that it is a "touchstone" to the apostles themselves (and therefore to Christ). A touchstone is something used to test the veracity or purity of a substance. Protestants believe that this is exactly what God gave us as our sole infallible rule of faith. No pope necessary.

BECAUSE CATHOLICISM IS TRUE,

The papacy was established by Christ, has endured, and retains the authority entrusted to it by Christ, even to this day.

The historical fact of the papacy throughout every Christian century makes a compelling case that it was intended to be a perpetual office within the institution that Christ built.[5] The pope presided over or sent his legates to ecumenical councils and confirmed (or refused confirmation) of their decisions, and members of the Church accepted these decrees as binding.

But what is the evidence that Peter was in Rome and established a church there? First, while the Bible does not explicitly say "Peter was the bishop of Rome," in Peter's first epistle he ends by saying, "She who is at Babylon, who is like-

wise chosen, sends you greetings; and so does my son Mark"
(1 Pet. 5:13). We know from its usage in the book of Revelation that Babylon was a code word for Rome. Peter chose to
be subtle here, since the Christians were being persecuted in
Rome, and he, its leader, had to be careful. While this does not
prove Peter was in Rome, it is biblical evidence for the claim.

Several early Christians testify to the existence of the bishop of Rome, from Peter onward. In the 100s, Irenaeus spoke
of the church in Rome founded by the apostles Peter and
Paul and went on to describe the succession of bishops from
there:

> The blessed apostles, then, having founded and built up
> the Church, committed into the hands of Linus the office
> of the episcopate. Of this Linus, Paul makes mention in
> the Epistles to Timothy. To him succeeded Anacletus; and
> after him, in the third place from the apostles, Clement was
> allotted the bishopric.[6]

The Clement mentioned at the end of this passage is the author of a first-century letter to the church in Corinth. Clement begins the letter by stating that he writes from the church
in Rome, strengthening the claim that this line of bishops
dwelled in Rome and was begun by Peter. Ignatius of Antioch, Tertullian, Eusebius, Jerome, and John Chrysostom,
among others, testify to the historical reality of Peter's so-
journ and martyrdom in Rome. An unbiased examination
of the historical evidence, coupled with Peter's words in his
first epistle, make an overwhelming case for the first bishop
of Rome being Peter and the line continuing in unbroken
succession.

But what about Scripture being a touchstone to the apostles? A Catholic can happily agree that it is indeed that. But

that does not mean that Scripture is the *sole* touchstone to the apostles. St. Paul tells us in his letter to the church in Ephesus that God built his Church on human beings:

> So then you are no longer strangers and sojourners, but you are fellow citizens with the saints and members of the household of God, built upon the foundation of the apostles and prophets, Christ Jesus himself being the cornerstone.[7]

Christ is the ultimate foundation, and he chose the apostles as the foundational layer for the Church. These are men and therefore, it is true, open to corruption. But God by his power protected these men from error in their teachings, which even Protestants believe—for they accept the scriptures written by these men.

God provided us multiple touchstones to Christ: the apostles and their successors (the magisterium), the Apostolic Tradition, and Sacred Scripture.

THE PROTESTANT'S DILEMMA

If Protestantism is true, then after 1,500 years of having a bishop of Rome called the prince of the apostles, the successor of Peter to whom Christ gave the keys to the kingdom of heaven (cf. Matt. 16:19), God eradicated the office of the papacy. No longer would his Church have a leader, a "servant of the servants of God."[8] Instead, God left his Church to follow whatever leaders declared themselves to be so in whatever churches they founded on the basis of their own authority or personal revelations.

3

ECUMENICAL COUNCILS

IF PROTESTANTISM IS TRUE,

Ecumenical councils somehow no longer have the authority they used to have.

For the first several centuries of the Church's existence, bishops gathered in councils to define true doctrines and condemn heresies, issuing decrees that were recognized as binding upon all the faithful. But at a certain point in history, these councils must somehow have ceased to carry that universal teaching authority. Instead they became mere ceremonial gatherings of the Church's bishops—or worse, cabals of an apostate church taken over by traditions of men.

The Protestant Conception of Ecumenical Councils

Protestants contend that no council of the Church, even the ones traditionally deemed ecumenical (universal), carry any authority—except insofar as they accurately interpret Scripture, in which case the authority is the Bible's, not theirs. Thus the first four councils of the Church, which largely answered trinitarian and christological questions, are considered "authoritative" only insofar as they are accurate deductions from the words of God in the Bible. Most Protestants allege, however, that even these early councils contained errors. For example, few are willing to accept that Mary is the "mother of God," as the third ecumenical council in Ephesus declared. Even Martin Luther, who had no problem with this title, contended that Church councils in general contained errors, as he revealed in his famous concluding remarks at the Diet of Worms:

> Unless I am convinced by the testimony of the Scripture or by clear reason (for I do not trust either in the pope or in councils alone, since it is well known that they have often erred and contradicted themselves), I am bound by Scripture I have quoted and my conscience is captive to the word of God.

Luther here presents the accepted Protestant belief that ecumenical councils have erred and "contradicted themselves" by deviating from the true meaning of God's word as found in the Bible. The Westminster Confession of Faith, the most important confessional document of Calvinist (or Reformed) Protestantism, echoes Luther's distrust of Church councils:

> All synods or councils since the apostles' times, whether general [ecumenical] or particular, may err, and many have erred; therefore they are not to be made the rule of faith or practice, but to be used as a help in both.[9]

Instead, the Bible alone is to be the sole authoritative rule of faith within Protestantism. This is the doctrine known as *sola scriptura*, which we will explore in greater depth later.

More traditional Protestants of the Anglican or Reformed communities, however, do view the first four councils as authoritative. They contend that for a council to be considered an ecumenical (and therefore authoritative) one, it had to have been attended by all five major patriarchs (bishops of important cities or areas): those of Rome, Constantinople, Antioch, Alexandria, and Jerusalem. They claim that the first four councils met this criterion. But, they argue, due to the divisions that have occurred in the Church since—notably the Coptic and Eastern Orthodox schisms—it has become impossible for these five patriarchs to be present at a council, making ecumenical councils a practical impossibility to this day.

BECAUSE CATHOLICISM IS TRUE,

Church councils have the same binding authority today that they did in the early centuries.

The Church has held ecumenical councils since the apostolic age (first century). We see the precedent and pattern for these councils in Acts 15, the Council of Jerusalem. The Church was posed with the question of whether Gentile converts to the Christian faith needed to be circumcised in order to be saved. In preparation for the council, Paul and Barnabas "had no small dissension and debate with them [Judaizers]," and so they were "appointed to go up to Jerusalem to the apostles and the elders about this question [of circumcision]" (Acts 15:2).

After much debate among the apostles and elders, Peter stood and explained how God gave the Holy Spirit to the Gentiles, and that salvation comes by grace through faith—not by following the Mosaic Law. The apostles then drafted a letter, to be sent out to the churches, in which the men making these challenges were rebuked as having gone out *without the authority of the apostles*. The decisions made by the council were decreed, beginning with the authoritative formula, "It has seemed good to the Holy Spirit and to us." Protestants recognize the authority of this council because the apostles themselves led it. Also, the council is recorded in the Bible, so its prescriptions are authoritative for that reason.

The first ecumenical council to be convened was at Nicaea in the year 325. It was attended by more than 300 bishops, including Hosius, bishop of Cordova and Pope Sylvester's representative (or "legate"). The primary purpose of the council was to determine whether the teachings of Arius, a deacon from Alexandria who denied the divinity of Christ and his consubstantial relationship with God the Father, were heresy. The truths of Christ's divinity and of his consubstantiality ("same substance" or "one in being") with the Father were consequently confirmed as dogmas. Protestants accept the decrees of this council and even point to it as being *the* standard for Trinitarian orthodoxy. Most Protestants today still recite the Nicene Creed, the first part of which was formulated at Nicaea.

They also accept the second ecumenical council, held in Constantinople in the year 381, which dogmatically affirmed the truth of the Holy Spirit's divinity, condemning the heresy of Macedonius. The second half of the Creed was drawn up at this council, and the vast majority of Protestants proudly recite it as a profession of their most fundamental beliefs.

The First Council of Ephesus in the year 431 was the third ecumenical council, which condemned Nestorius's belief that Mary was the mother only of Christ's human nature. Such a notion would have mortally wounded the true theology of the Incarnation, making it impossible to say that "God died on the cross for our sins." The fourth ecumenical council occurred in Chalcedon in the year 451, rejecting monophysitism—the belief that Christ had only one nature—and affirming that Jesus had two natures in one person.

These councils establish the basis for Trinitarian and Christological orthodoxy that is followed by almost all Protestants. In fact, Protestants believe that anyone who rejects these truths puts himself outside of Christianity (a major reason why they consider Mormons non-Christians). Thus Protestants desire to affirm these councils as authoritative. Yet the council in Ephesus also taught that Mary was the mother of God, a title that makes most Protestants uneasy. We'll tackle that issue in a later chapter, but the material point here is that these councils both defined orthodoxy and, in the eyes of Protestants, somehow also contained erroneous or questionable decrees.

More problems remain for Protestants who seek to accept the first four councils while rejecting others. The fifth ecumenical council, Constantinople II, declared that Mary remained a virgin her whole life, a belief strenuously rejected by most Protestants. Yet the next one, held in the seventh century, condemned the monothelite belief that Christ had only one will. It decreed that Christ had two wills—one divine and one human—a truth that Protestants believe as another essential component to Christological orthodoxy.

Answering the Protestant Objections

Does it make sense, as Protestants argue, that ecumenical councils are authoritative only insofar as they accurately represent scriptural truth? When we look at the Council of Jerusalem, we see that the Church settled the matter in question by reference to the *apostles' God-given authority within the Church* and not by reliance on the Old Testament (which was the only "Scripture" in existence at the time, with only a few epistles having been written to date and a settled canon still many years away[10]). Indeed, the Old Testament was at best unclear on the matter, both requiring circumcision[11] and foreshadowing Gentile salvation.[12] So the claim that councils are authoritative only when they agree with Scripture—by which the Reformers meant both Old and New Testaments—makes little sense when applied to this prototypical council.

But there's a second problem with this theory. Who has the authority to accurately interpret the scriptures (and therefore rule whether a council affirms or contradicts their truths)? Luther believed that *he* did. Other Protestants claimed that Luther erred and that *they* had the correct key to Scripture's meaning. The problem of varying Protestant interpretations of biblical truth persists to this day. Without a standard for interpreting Scripture, then, according to this test it's impossible to say with certainty whether a given council teaches authoritatively.

What about the five-patriarch theory (also known as the "pentarchy"): that the presence of the major patriarchs was the necessary criterion for an ecumenical council? The Emperor Justinian I favored this model of the governance of Christendom, where the five patriarchs of the major sees would all belong to one empire. In the late 600s, the council of Trullo (which has never been accepted as authoritative by the Catholic Church) attempted to lend credence to the pentarchy theory by ranking the five patriarchal sees.

But using this theory as a criterion for recognizing the first ecumenical councils is problematic. For starters, there was no patriarch of Constantinople in the year 325 during the first Nicene council, so the theory is disproven from the outset. Further, the ecumenical council in Ephesus in the year 431 condemned Nestorius, who *was* the patriarch of Constantinople. Similarly, the ecumenical council in Chalcedon in the year 451 condemned Dioscorus, the patriarch of Alexandria, as a heretic. But Dioscorus rejected the excommunication and is recognized by the Coptic Church as a pope. When patriarchs break in schism, the pentarchy theory does not provide a rule for knowing which side is orthodox and which is schismatic.

In truth, this theory was a historical convenience invented by the Byzantine emperor in the hopes of keeping order in his empire. Modern Protestants have taken up the theory as an objective way of identifying authoritative councils; but, as we have seen, it simply doesn't work.

The Catholic Criterion for an Ecumenical Council

If none of the Protestant theories makes sense, what makes a council ecumenical and thus authoritative? Quite simply: the pope.

The bishop of Rome is the successor of Peter, to whom Christ gave the "keys to the kingdom of heaven" as well as the authority to bind and loose (cf. Matt. 16:18–19). Accordingly, during these early councils we find the other patriarchs showing great deference to the pope. For instance, leading up to the Council of Chalcedon in 451—which established Christ as both fully God and fully human—Flavian, the patriarch of Constantinople, wrote the pope about the extremity of the current religious-political conflict and called for his intervention:

When I began to appeal to the throne of the Apostolic See of Peter, the Prince of the apostles, and to the whole sacred synod, which is obedient to Your Holiness, at once a crowd of soldiers surrounded me and barred my way when I wished to take refuge at the holy altar. . . . Therefore, I beseech Your Holiness not to permit these things to be treated with indifference . . . but to rise up first on behalf of the cause of our orthodox Faith, now destroyed by un-

lawful acts. . . . Further to issue an authoritative instruction
. . . so that a like faith may everywhere be preached by the
assembly of a united synod of fathers, both Eastern and
Western. Thus the laws of the fathers may prevail and all
that has been done amiss be rendered null and void. Bring
healing to this ghastly wound.[13]

The acts of the council of Chalcedon likewise speak forceful-
ly for Pope Leo's primacy and authority:

Wherefore the most holy and blessed Leo, archbishop of
the great and elder Rome, through us, and through this
present most holy synod together with the thrice-blessed
and all-glorious Peter the Apostle, who is the Rock and
foundation of the Catholic Church, and the foundation of
the orthodox faith, hath stripped him [Dioscorus, Patriarch
of Alexandria] of his episcopate, and hath alienated from
him all hieratic worthiness.[14]

The bishop of Rome is, by God's grace, the final guarantor of
orthodoxy. Even when the bishops of the other major sees fell
into heresy (for example, during the Arian crisis in the third
and fourth centuries), the pope did not. The only criterion
for a council to be considered ecumenical that makes historical sense is the approval of the pope. Even in the council of
Jerusalem in the book of Acts, we see that Peter is the first to
speak and declare the orthodox belief, a foreshadowing of the
role of the bishops of Rome in later councils.

The Catholic Church is the only Christian Church or
community that still holds ecumenical councils today. No
other group dares to claim that it has held one, which makes
sense when you realize that no other group is led by the bishop of Rome.

THE PROTESTANT'S DILEMMA

Protestants claim they unquestioningly accept the authority of the first four ecumenical councils, which declared the foundational truths of Christianity. Yet they reject certain decrees even of those councils and accept certain decrees from *later* councils while rejecting others. And they do not have a rule for determining why the first four are ecumenical but later ones are not. Assuming the Catholic Church is wrong about what makes a council ecumenical, why did God design his Church such that, for centuries, these councils were the primary way in which vitally important matters of the Faith were discerned and authoritatively proclaimed, but then *remove* his authority from them such that they could no longer be trustworthy?

4

THE FOUR MARKS
OF THE CHURCH

IF PROTESTANTISM IS TRUE,

The meaning of the four marks of the Church fundamentally changed during the Reformation.

Based upon the promises made by Christ, the four marks[15] of the Church are encapsulated in the fourth-century Nicene Creed: "We believe in one, holy, catholic, and apostolic Church." The Protestant Reformers found themselves in the awkward position of having to affirm this ancient creed—understood as the measure of Christian ecclesiology—while still maintaining their new conception of the Church. The only way Protestantism can reconcile the two is to assert that the four marks no longer mean what they used to.

Protestantism's Interpretation of the Four Marks

Protestants understand the Church to be "one" only in the sense that the collections of Christians that make up the invisible Church all form one group. Since the Holy Spirit dwells within every Christian, together they form the one group of true believers. In this way, the Church is not a unified, visible body but an invisible collection of disconnected parts (though Protestants do look ahead to a future unification of the body upon Christ's return).

Regarding the second mark—that the Church is holy—traditional Protestant doctrine states that holiness comes from Christ's *imputing* his righteousness to the Christian. Thus the Father legally declares a Christian to be holy on behalf of Christ's righteousness, but he is not actually made holy. This Protestant understanding of holiness for the individual Christian is then applied to the Church in general: through Christ, the Church is *declared* holy because his righteousness is imputed to it collectively.

Martin Luther reveals the Protestant conception of the first two marks when discussing his interpretation of the parallel passage found in the Apostles' Creed:

> If these words had been used in the Creed: "I believe that there is a holy Christian people," it would have been easy to avoid all the misery that has come in with this blind, obscure word "church"; for the term "Christian, holy people" would have brought along with it, clearly and powerfully, both understanding and the judgment on the question "What is and what is not a church?" One who heard the words "Christian, holy people" would have been able to decide off-hand, "The pope is not a people, still less a holy Christian people." So, too, the bishops, priests, and monks are not a holy Christian people, for they do not believe in Christ, do not lead holy lives, and are the devil's wicked, shameful people.[16]

Luther shows his disdain for the traditional conception of the Church and offers his own opinion as preferable: The Church is merely the people who believe in Jesus, and so they are holy because of their faith.

At first blush, it would seem that affirming that the Church is "catholic" would be exceedingly difficult for Protestants. But actually this mark is explained easily under the Protestant paradigm. Since, they say, the root meaning of *catholic* is "universal," and since they believe that Christ's Church is universal in scope—open to every person in the world—they can happily proclaim that they believe the Church is catholic with a lowercase "c."

For the fourth mark, many Protestant communities claim to be apostolic in that they teach the same truth that God gave to the apostles in the first century. Because (they say) their community's interpretation of the Bible is the same as the apostles', their church is "apostolic."

BECAUSE CATHOLICISM IS TRUE,

The four marks of the Church have the same meaning today as they did when the early Christians formulated the Creed.

The first mark, that the Church is *one*, means that it is visibly unified and professes the same faith. Your body is a visible unity, more than just a mere collection of parts stuck together, and so is Christ's. St. Paul exhorts us to this unity in his letter to the Ephesians:

> I therefore, a prisoner for the Lord, beg you to lead a life worthy of the calling to which you have been called . . . forbearing one another in love, eager to maintain the unity of the Spirit in the bond of peace. There is one body and one Spirit, just as you were called to the one hope that

belongs to your call, one Lord, one faith, one baptism, one God and Father of us all, who is above all and through all and in all.[17]

Protestantism, with its cacophony of competing voices and communities, cannot claim to profess "one faith," but the Catholic Church can. Its magisterium is able to declare what is true and what is false, drawing the bounds of orthodox belief. The first few councils of the Church, which formulated this creed, by their very existence demonstrate the working of this teaching authority to decree the one faith of the Church, to which all Christians must adhere (or else be in heresy). The councils convened to address novel teachings that ran counter to the one Faith believed by the Church since apostolic times, and they set out to correct those errors so that the faithful might remain unified in the truth.

As for the second mark, that the Church is holy, the Catholic Church teaches that Christians become *truly* holy because God gives them grace, which is divine life. Once again, we find evidence for this belief in Ephesians:

Husbands, love your wives, as Christ loved the church and gave himself up for her, that he might sanctify her, having cleansed her by the washing of water with the word, that he might present the church to himself in splendor, without spot or wrinkle or any such thing, that she might be holy and without blemish.[18]

Notice that Paul nowhere claims that God only declares the Church to be holy, but rather that Christ really cleanses it, sanctifies it, and presents it without blemish to himself. In Catholic theology, following the biblical pattern, Christ has married his Church, and so he truly purifies it. Christ did not give himself up for the Church just so God could declare a legal fiction that it is pure. Instead, his sacrifice of love is powerful enough to truly cleanse it in truth.

The third mark, that the Church is catholic, indeed speaks of its universality, but not in the rather superficial way Protestants do. As the *Catechism of the Catholic Church* explains:

> The word "catholic" means "universal," in the sense of "according to the totality" or "in keeping with the whole." The Church is catholic in a double sense: first, the Church is catholic because Christ is present in her. "Where there is Christ Jesus, there is the Catholic Church." In her subsists the fullness of Christ's body united with its head; this implies that she receives from him "the fullness of the means of salvation" which he has willed: correct and complete confession of faith, full sacramental life, and ordained ministry in apostolic succession. The Church was, in this fundamental sense, catholic on the day of Pentecost and will always be so until the day of the Parousia.[19]

This full meaning of the word *catholic* was understood in the early 100s, as evidenced by the letter of Ignatius, bishop of Antioch, to the Smyrnaeans:

> See that you all follow the bishop, even as Jesus Christ does the Father, and the presbytery as you would the apostles; and reverence the deacons, as being the institution of God. Let no man do anything connected with the Church without the bishop. Let that be deemed a proper Eucharist, which is [administered] either by the bishop, or by one to whom he has entrusted it. Wherever the bishop shall appear, there let the multitude [of the people] also be; even as, wherever Jesus Christ is, there is the Catholic Church.

It is not lawful without the bishop either to baptize or to celebrate a love-feast; but whatsoever he shall approve of, that is also pleasing to God, so that everything that is done may be secure and valid.[20]

In this chapter of his epistle, we see the affirmation of the threefold hierarchy of bishop, priest, and deacon, as well as the proper context for the celebration of the Eucharist and baptism. The early Church saw these aspects as essential to the Church's catholicity, a true universality that included the ordained leaders and the sacraments.

The fourth mark, apostolicity, indicates that the Church is built on the foundation of the apostles, with Christ as the cornerstone: "So then you are no longer strangers and sojourners, but you are fellow citizens with the holy ones and members of the household of God, built upon the foundation of the apostles and prophets, with Christ Jesus himself as the capstone" (Eph. 2:19–20). (The "household of God" is the Church: see Heb. 3:4–6.) To have a church built upon an apostolic foundation means not merely to be in (presumed) doctrinal agreement or moral unity with the apostles—it means to be sharers in the apostles' authority. God transmitted that authority from the apostles to their successors, the bishops, through the laying on of hands—and then in turn to their successors (cf. 1 Tim. 4:14). Through this *apostolic* succession these bishops remain the foundation of the apostolic Church.

We find this understanding as early as the second century in the writings of Irenaeus, bishop of Lyons:

Wherefore it is incumbent to obey the presbyters who are in the Church—those who, as I have shown, possess the succession from the apostles; those who, together with the succession of the episcopate, have received the certain gift of truth, according to the good pleasure of the Father. But [it is also incumbent] to hold in suspicion others who depart from the primitive succession, and assemble themselves together in any place whatsoever, [looking upon them] either as heretics of perverse minds, or as schismatics puffed up and self-pleasing, or again as hypocrites, acting thus for the sake of lucre and vainglory. For all these have fallen from the truth.[21]

The Protestant idea of apostolicity is a half-truth. It does mean unity of belief with apostolic teaching; however, the way that we know what the apostles taught is not to exercise our personal judgment but to look to their successors, to whom apostolic faith and authority have been given.

THE PROTESTANT'S DILEMMA

If Protestantism is true, then the Protestant Reformers had the authority to change the meaning of the four marks to align them with their novel doctrines about the Church. Their actions show how easily people can rationalize inconsistencies between their beliefs and the historical evidence by creating new definitions for statements. What is to stop someone else from reinterpreting other parts of the Creed to conform to *his* new ideas?

5

PROTESTANTISM'S VIEW OF THE CATHOLIC CHURCH

IF PROTESTANTISM IS TRUE,

Catholics are at best in serious error, and at worst non-Christian cultists.

Protestants are a diverse lot doctrinally, and some are more liturgical than others, but no Protestant community comes close to embracing Catholicism's vast array of "extrabiblical" prayers, practices, and teachings. Because of this, if Protestants are being consistent with their beliefs, they can't view Catholics as fellow Christians fighting the good fight; rather, they must conclude that Catholics are idolatrous apostates.

Protestant Perspectives on Catholicism

Some Fundamentalist groups do indeed identify the pope as the Antichrist and the Catholic Church as the "whore of Babylon" mentioned in Revelation 17 and 18. And it's not just Protestants on that extreme end of the spectrum who think this way. In the section on the papacy, we saw that the Westminster Confession of Faith—the most important document for the Reformed movement of Protestantism—named the pope as the Antichrist.

That said, many modern Protestants, including Bible-believing Evangelicals, take a softer stance toward Catholicism. They see it as a mildly corrupted form of biblical Christianity but still a legitimately Christian faith whose members sincerely believe in Jesus. Protestant author and speaker John Armstrong warmly describes this view of the Catholic Church:

> If Christ is truly the center ... [i]t means I can no longer be an anti-Catholic, evangelical (Reformed) Protestant. With deep conviction, I am compelled to regard both Catholics and the Catholic Church with love and esteem. This personal commitment to oneness has enabled me to draw great blessings from the Catholic tradition and develop many wonderful friendships with Catholic brothers and sisters in Christ.[22]

But Protestants of all stripes *should* get up in arms when faced with the spectacle of Catholics kneeling in worship of a consecrated communion host. No Protestant, however much he may protest to believe Jesus is present in some way, can justify adoring bread and wine. He must conclude that Catholics commit the sin of idolatry.

Although Catholics believe in the Trinity, Protestants should likewise balk at their elevation of the Virgin Mary above all other creatures, especially in the doctrines of her Assumption and her sinless life. They believe that Jesus alone lived a sinless life, so Mary's achieving the same feat can't help but steal glory from God, to whom belongs all glory and praise.

Such distinctively Catholic beliefs stem from recognizing Sacred Tradition as a source of divine revelation equal to

Scripture. This too should disturb any Protestant, for whom the Bible alone is God's authoritative word. Any "tradition" outside of Scripture can be only a tradition of men.

BECAUSE CATHOLICISM IS TRUE,

Catholics are Christians in the fullest sense.

A paradox is presented when trying to match up the Catholic Church against the caricatures and accusations thrown at it. On the one hand, those today who call the pope Antichrist have been able to witness recent popes heroically defending the core tenets of Christianity against virulent modern attacks. The beloved disciple, St. John, tells us how to know who the Antichrist is: "Who is the liar but he who denies that Jesus is the Christ? This is the antichrist, he who denies the Father and the Son" (1 John 2:22). But we can see with our own eyes examples of popes who never stop proclaiming that Jesus is the Christ, our savior, the only begotten Son of the Father. So by the biblical definition, the pope cannot be the Antichrist.

Likewise, the Catholic Church is thought to elevate Mary too much, yet the Protestant Reformers, as we shall see in a later section, retained Marian doctrines and defended them against their fellow Protestants. They realized that these beliefs were well-grounded in Scripture and in the early Church's faith.

Throughout this book we will examine in more detail specific areas in which the Church can be shown to profess the fullness of Christian truth. But the basic fact to remember here is that the Catholic Church, when faced with a decision to hold to the ancient Faith or adopt a novelty, has in every case chosen the former. Rather than seeing in the Church the characteristic marks of the devil, which would cause it to be "tossed back and forth and carried about with every wind of doctrine" (Eph. 4:14) and adopt idolatrous practices and beliefs, we recognize how it has remained true to the teachings of Christ and the apostles.

THE PROTESTANT'S DILEMMA

If Protestantism is true, then Catholicism can only be viewed as serious, perhaps even diabolical, idolatry. Yet the marks the Bible tells us to look for to identify falsehoods and deceit are absent from the Catholic Church. Instead, Catholicism's hallmark is that of a stalwart witness to Jesus Christ.

6

DOCTRINAL RELIABILITY

IF PROTESTANTISM IS TRUE,

We're stuck without a trustworthy guide to Christian truth.

The Catholic Church makes the *outlandish* claim that all its teachings on faith and morals are true—that not a single one of them is erroneous. As a Protestant, when I learned about this claim, I smelled blood in the water. I knew that there was no way it could be true, and that all I had to do was find *one* example of a false teaching and the whole house of Catholic cards would come tumbling down. Why was I so sure that the Catholic Church's claim was false? Simple: I knew from human experience that every person and human institution is corrupt in some way.

Every Person and "Church" is Fallible

St. Paul writes, "[A]ll have sinned and fallen short of the glory of God" because "there is none righteous, no not one" (Rom. 3:23). Every organization and institution is therefore full of people who sin. Churches aren't exempt: How many pastors have been caught in infidelities, embezzlement, and worse? If they sin, they can err, too. As a Protestant, although I thought what my pastor taught was mostly true, I didn't necessarily agree with everything he taught. Why should I? He was just another sinful, fallible human being like me.

Furthermore, as a Protestant I believed that the Bible taught that we had no hope of ever becoming righteous. By faith, Christ's righteousness is *imputed* to us by the Father such that we appear holy, but deep down we remain sinful and corrupted people. My Protestant friends and mentors loved Isaiah 64:6, where, speaking of the Israelites, the prophet says: "We have all become like one who is unclean, and all our righteous deeds are like a polluted garment."

Filthy rags and polluted garments: That's what human goodness amounts to.

Given the universal corruption in people and in institutions, what hubris for the Catholic Church to claim that it teaches no error! Protestant churches, I thought, are at least honest enough to recognize their fallibility. They know the Bible is true and they try to teach from the Bible—if sometimes they teach contradictory things from it, well, that's a result of their corruption. Protestants have to give their churches only qualified or conditional assent, knowing that at any time they could leave to find one whose doctrines were less corrupted.

BECAUSE CATHOLICISM IS TRUE,

The Church is both a human institution and a supernatural society, with Christ at the head.

Infallibility is a practical necessity for Christianity, because it safeguards the deposit of faith given by Christ to the apostles and first Christians. Imagine if God didn't protect the Church from error: We would be left to our own devices to identify and preserve what Jesus taught. After 2,000 years of such fallible human activity, and the countless disagreements and divisions it inevitably produces, we could have little expectation that what was passed down to us was the pristine truth of divine revelation.

A bald-faced appeal to the Holy Spirit's help doesn't solve the problem, either, since the *way* in which the Spirit works would have to be given. For Protestants, the Holy Spirit primarily works within individual Christians; but the ubiquitous fractures among them make it impossible to conclude that the Holy Spirit is leading *all* of them to truth. The Holy Spirit *could* work infallibly to guide someone into the full truth of revelation, but there's no sure way for a Protestant to say where this has happened. What practical good is that guidance if we can't identify it?

Yet Protestants subconsciously realize the need for infallibility, through their recognition that, by inspiring fallible men to write the books of Scripture, God ensured that what was written was free from all error. Without that belief, it would make no sense to call Scripture the rule of faith for Christians, since it *could* present mere human ideas as divine truth. But they stop short of recognizing an infallible guide to *interpreting* Scripture—and so every fallible Protestant must do it himself as best as he is able, fashioning his own body of fallible doctrines to believe in.

As I continued growing in my faith and sought to refute the wild Catholic claim of infallibility, I was still bothered by the lack of unity among Christians, which was clearly against Christ's and Paul's commands. I investigated where we got the books of the Bible and looked at moral issues such as contraception—which I had always assumed was a good thing—where the Catholic Church contrasted with Protestantism. I found reasonable answers to my old objections and challenged my Evangelical friends with them (my argument against contraception must have felt like a bolt of lightning out of the sky), and they failed to respond with convincing answers.

I remember the day I could see that the Catholic Church's claim of infallibility *just might be true.* It was similar to when I had been an atheist and one day realized that *Jesus Christ might really be who he said he was.* It was exhilarating! It meant that God had not left us alone to wallow in error. It also meant that I could actually *become* holy! Though "all" sinned and fell short of God's glory, Jesus did not; this meant that we too could live in true freedom from the slavery of sin. Likewise, even though the Church is made up of sinful human beings, the Holy Spirit could make it not just infallible but also holy.

As a Protestant I believed that God infallibly guided sinful men to write inerrant, divine truth: the Bible. It was only one step further also to believe that throughout time God continued to guide fallible men into all truth.

THE PROTESTANT'S DILEMMA

If Protestantism is true, then Christian churches are no more reliable than any other human institution. Any confidence we place in a set of doctrines, therefore, is shaky; we must always take a stand with one foot out the door. Without the assurance that God has preserved the deposit of faith from error and by his Spirit guided people in every age to defend that truth, we who live two millennia after Jesus Christ cannot trust with certainty what we have been taught about him. We're left to sift through the sparse rubble of (allegedly) historical documents and piece together a puzzle for which we don't have the complete picture. We surely believe that God would never leave us in such a state; but if Protestantism is true, he has.

PART II

THE
BIBLE
AND
TRADITION

7

MARTIN LUTHER AND THE CANON

IF PROTESTANTISM IS TRUE,

It's okay to remove books from the New Testament canon if you judge them to be non-inspired.

The canon of the New Testament slowly took shape over the first 300 years of Christianity. Some books, like the four Gospels, were widely accepted early on, whereas others were doubted by many for a long time. But by the fifth century, the New Testament canon of twenty-seven books was firmly settled. In spite of this, over a thousand years later, Martin Luther dismissed four of those books when he translated the New Testament into German.

Four on the Chopping Block

Martin Luther was excommunicated in the year 1521.[23] The following year, he published his German New Testament but relegated four of the books to the end with this preface: "Up to this point we have had to do with the true and certain chief books of the New Testament. The four which follow have from ancient times had a different reputation."[24] Hebrews, James, Jude, and Revelation were the books whose inspiration he rejected.

Here is an excerpt from his introduction to James and Jude:

> I do not regard it as the writing of an apostle; and my reasons follow. In the first place it is flatly against Paul and all the rest of Scripture in ascribing justification to works. . . . This fault, therefore, proves that this epistle is not the work of any apostle. . . . But this James does nothing more than drive to the law and to its works. . . . He mangles the Scriptures and thereby opposes Paul and all Scripture. . . . Therefore, I will not have him in my Bible to be numbered among the true chief books.
>
> Concerning the epistle of Jude, no one can deny that it is an extract or copy of Peter's second epistle, so very like it are all the words. He also speaks of the apostles like a disciple who comes long after them and cites sayings and incidents that are found nowhere else in the Scriptures.[25]

So Luther submitted the books of the Bible to his own doctrine and found them incompatible with it.[26] He also judged that Jude was merely a modified copy of 2 Peter, and added his opinion that its unique sayings are further reason to reject it. Luther excoriated Revelation as well, denying that an apostle wrote it or that the Holy Spirit inspired it.[27] These four books were placed in an appendix in an effort to drop them from the New Testament entirely.

BECAUSE CATHOLICISM IS TRUE,

God guided the early Church to discern the New Testament, and no man afterward can change it.

It might appear at first that Luther was merely trying to be historically accurate in rejecting these books, since three of the four were not universally accepted early on in the Church. However, it is clear that Luther denied the inspiration of these books primarily for theological, not historical, reasons. Sure, the early doubts about these books made his claims more palatable. But in truth, these books either contained teachings that directly contradicted the novel doctrines he was proposing (like *sola fide*), or he simply did not think much of them.

If he had rejected them for purely historical reasons, he should have also rejected 2 Peter and 2 and 3 John, which were also not universally attested to in the first centuries of the Church. But he didn't reject those, because he didn't find anything in them that disagreed with his own theological opinions. His solution was to override historical concerns altogether and appeal to no authority but his own personal discernment. Even though this particular assertion of Luther's did not carry the day, the majority of his opinions did catch on with the Protestant Reformation as a whole and formed the basis for its common doctrines.

THE PROTESTANT'S DILEMMA

If Protestantism is true, then there is no reason why someone today could not remove any number of books from the New Testament and declare that he has come up with the true Bible, made up of whichever books coincide with his beliefs. After all, the father of the Protestant Reformation did just that to a thousand-year-old canon.

8
—
THE DEUTEROCANONICAL BOOKS

IF PROTESTANTISM IS TRUE,

God allowed the early Church to put seven books in the Bible that didn't belong there.

As we saw in the previous section, Martin Luther was not afraid to challenge the canon of Scripture. Though his alteration of the New Testament ultimately wasn't adopted by all of the Protestant movements, his alteration of the Old Testament *was*, and by the end of the Reformation, Protestantism had removed seven books (the deuterocanonicals) from the Old Testament canon.

Protestants Reject the Deuterocanonicals

The Protestants rejected these books for two main reasons. The first was a problematic passage in 2 Maccabees, and the second was their desire to go "back to the sources," which in this case meant using the same books that the Jews ultimately decided upon. 2 Maccabees included a laudatory reference to prayers for the dead—a teaching that had been encouraged in the Catholic Church for the souls in purgatory. Recall Luther's protest against the sale of indulgences to remove the temporal punishment due for already forgiven sins—punishment that must be paid before a soul would be fit to enter heaven. Luther and the Reformers rejected purgatory, so all that was connected with it also had to go: indulgences, prayers for the dead, and the communion of saints (which includes those both living and asleep in Christ).

The Reformers pointed out that these seven books were not included in the Jewish Hebrew Bible. Some Protestant apologists seek to bolster this claim by mentioning the theory that, around the year 90, a council of Jews at a city called Jamnia explicitly rejected these books.[28] Others like to point out that some Church Fathers rejected one or more of these books. They strengthen this argument with the testimony of Josephus and Philo—two Jews from the first century—who also did not accept them.

BECAUSE CATHOLICISM IS TRUE,

Christ's Church, and not the Jews, possessed the authority and divine guidance to discern the Old Testament canon.

A little historical background is needed here. The first Greek translation of the Hebrew Old Testament, used during Jesus' time, was called the Septuagint. It was an evolving set of books that was added to from the third century B.C. until the time of Christ. It remains the most ancient translation of the Old Testament that we have today and so is used to correct the errors that crept into the Hebrew text, the oldest existing examples of which date only from the sixth century. It was used extensively in the Near East by rabbis, and in the first century the apostles quoted prophecies from it in the books that became the New Testament. It was accepted as authoritative by the Jews of Alexandria and then by all Jews in Greek-speaking countries.

By the time of Christ, the Septuagint contained the deuterocanonical books.

Historical evidence also shows that there were multiple, conflicting Jewish canons at the time of Christ. How could the Jews close their canon when they were still awaiting the advent of the new Elijah (John the Baptist) and the new Moses (Jesus)? Thus the argument that Christians should base their Old Testament off of the Hebrew Bible rather than the Greek Septuagint is dubious.[29]

Still, some say, should we be reading books as canonical to the Hebrew Bible if they weren't written in Hebrew? Well, some of the seven deuterocanonical books were originally written in Hebrew and only later translated into Greek and other languages. Sirach and parts of Baruch are two such books, and an Aramaic version of Tobit was found in the Dead Sea Scrolls.[30] In the nineteenth and twentieth centuries, Hebrew manuscripts of Sirach were found amounting to two-thirds of the entire work, including one pre-Christian manuscript.[31] These manuscripts had not been found at the time of the Protestant Reformation, and one might hope that Luther would have taken them into account. Their subsequent discovery, though, nonetheless cuts the legs out from under the objection that the seven deuterocanonical books should be excluded because they were not originally written in Hebrew.

Several other problems emerge from accepting as authoritative the (alleged) Jewish council's decision at Jamnia at the end of the first century. First, most scholars today doubt that any such council ever took place. But even if it did, would Jewish leaders possess the authority to make a decision binding upon the Christian Church? Those Jews who had accepted Christ had already become Christians. The remainder had no rightful authority to decide anything about divine truth, as that authority had passed to those filled with the Holy Spirit (like the apostles). The same goes for the opinions of Josephus and Philo.

Finally, it should be pointed out that Protestants seeking to defend their canon based on historical evidence, even if they are convinced they have found sufficient proof, run into the problem that nowhere in Scripture does it say that this is the way to know which books belong in the canon. Such a criterion for choosing the canon in fact contradicts *sola scriptura*, because it is an extra-biblical principle. A consistent Protestant argument for selecting the canon of Scripture, then, must itself come from Scripture (which would create a circular argument). Unfortunately (but certainly providentially), no such instructions from God exist. Authority is our only appeal.

Regarding some Church Fathers who doubted the deuterocanonical books, it is true that several rejected one or more of them or put them on a level lower than the rest of Scripture. But many, including those with doubts, quoted them as Scripture with no distinction from the rest of the Bible. The broader fact is that the testimony of the Fathers was not unanimous on the Old Testament canon. Even Jerome, the great biblical scholar, early in his career favored the Hebrew canon but then changed his mind and submitted his opinion to the wisdom of the Church, accepting the deuterocanonicals as Scripture.[32]

THE PROTESTANT'S DILEMMA

If Protestantism is true, then for 1,500 years all of Christianity used an Old Testament that contained seven fully disposable, possibly deceptive books that God did not inspire. He did, however, allow the early Church to designate these books as Sacred Scripture and derive false teachings such as purgatory from their contents. Eventually, God's chosen Reformer, Martin Luther, was able to straighten out this tragic error, even though his similar abridgement of the *New* Testament was a mistake.

9

A

SELF-AUTHENTICATING BIBLE?

IF PROTESTANTISM IS TRUE,

The canon of Scripture is subject to every Christian's personal discernment.

The Reformers were not unaware of the conundrum we treated in the previous chapter, and some of them—John Calvin was the most influential proponent of this theory—offered an alternative: the self-authenticating canon. It states that a true Christian can read a given book and easily tell whether it is inspired by God or not. The Holy Spirit dwelling within the Christian would witness to the book's inspiration.

Calvin's Confident Theory

This theory did away with the need for trusting the corrupted early Church or for tracing the messy history of the canon's development. Instead, you as a faithful Christian simply picked up your Bible, read the books, and listened for the inner witness of the Spirit telling you that the books were inspired by God. Similarly, you could theoretically pick up a non-canonical epistle or Gospel from the first or second century, read it, and note the absence of the Spirit's confirmation of its inspiration. As Calvin described it:

> But a most pernicious error widely prevails that Scripture has only so much weight as is conceded to it by the consent of the church. . . . It is utterly vain, then, to pretend that the power of judging Scripture so lies with the church and that its certainty depends upon churchly assent. Thus, while the church receives and gives its seal of approval to Scripture, it does not thereby render authentic what is otherwise doubtful or controversial. . . . As to their question— How can we be assured that this has sprung from God unless we have recourse to the decree of the church?—it is as if someone asked: Whence will we learn to distinguish light from darkness, white from black, sweet from bitter? Indeed, Scripture exhibits fully as clear evidence of its own truth as white and black things do of their color, or sweet and bitter things do of their taste. . . . those whom the Holy Spirit has inwardly taught truly rest upon Scripture, and Scripture indeed is self-authenticated.[33]

Calvin makes two claims here: first, that the Church does not give authority to Scripture but rather Scripture has authority by the fact that God inspired it; secondly, that a Christian can know the canon from the Holy Spirit's testimony within him, not by trusting a decision of the Church. Moreover, a Christian can know quite easily what is inspired and what is not, as easily as distinguishing "white from black, sweet from bitter."

BECAUSE CATHOLICISM IS TRUE,

God guided his Church, but does not guide every individual Christian, to correctly discern the canon.

Calvin's first claim—that the Church does not give Scripture its authority—has never been contested by the Catholic Church, the Orthodox churches, or any Christian. It is a straw man: The Church teaches that it *received* inspired texts from God (through human authors), and that God guided it in discerning which among many texts were truly inspired. The Church is thus the servant of written revelation and not its master.

Calvin's second claim has become the common answer from Protestants who can't concede that a corrupt Church selected the canon. There's an element of truth to it: Surely the Holy Spirit *does* witness to our souls when we read the Bible. But Calvin sets up a false dichotomy here: Either the Church, by discerning the canon, imagines itself in authority over Scripture, *or* the canon is self-evident to any Christian. Calvin replaces the belief that God guided *the Church* in selecting the canon with the belief that God guides *me* or *you* in selecting it. He forces his readers to choose between these options, but in fact they are both false.

There is no principled reason, in Scripture or elsewhere, to believe that God would guide me or you in this discernment but not the Church. Moreover, Calvin's subjective criterion for discerning the canon is surely impractical and unrealistic. How would a person seeking truth but not yet indwelt by the Holy Spirit know which books to read to find truth? What about a new Christian who had not learned to distinguish the inner voice of the Spirit from his own? At what point after his conversion would a Christian be considered ready to help define the canon? If two Christians disagreed, whose inner judgment would be used to arbitrate their dispute and identify the *real* canon?

Another problem with Calvin's claim is that the facts of history flatly contradict it. As we have seen, the selection of the canon was not an easy, debate-free process that ended with the close of written revelation in the early second century. Rather, the canon emerged slowly through a laborious process, with differing canons being proposed by different Church Fathers during these centuries. If the canon were obvious and self-evident, the Holy Spirit would have led each of them to the same canon. Yet even these faithful, Spirit-filled men, so close to the time of the apostles and Christ himself, proposed different canons. It was not until almost A.D. 400 that the canon was settled, and it contained the seventy-three books of the Catholic Bible. When, more than 1,100 years later, the Reformers changed the canon by rejecting the seven deuterocanonical books (and Luther unsuccessfully tried to discard others) it was another example of intelligent and well-meaning Christians disagreeing about the "self-authenticated" canon.

THE PROTESTANT'S DILEMMA

If Protestantism is true, then the books of the canon are obvious just from reading them—at least to any true Christian bright enough to discern black from white. (Apparently that excludes Martin Luther, the founder of the Protestant Reformation, since he wanted to jettison four books from the New Testament.) Of course, this makes the canon contingent on the subjective opinions of millions of individual Christians, each of whom would have to personally figure out what it's supposed to be. It also creates a vicious circle, if: a) true Christians can tell in their hearts what the books of the Bible are, but b) the Bible is the only thing we have to tell us what true Christianity is. Without a trustworthy canon to tell us what true Christianity is, how can we know that we are true Christians able to discern what the canon is?

10

IDENTIFYING THE CANON

IF PROTESTANTISM IS TRUE,

The Bible is a "fallible collection of infallible books."

The historical realities of the canon of Scripture leave Protestants in a pickle. How can they know with certainty that the sixty-six books in their Bibles are *the* correct set of inspired books? They need to know with the strongest certainty possible, because they hold to *sola scriptura*—that from the Bible alone comes all of the saving truths that God revealed for man to believe and live by. But if they're not certain that the books contained in their Bible are all inspired by God, then those truths become open for debate; likewise, if they can't say for sure that they haven't left out some inspired books, then they face the possibility that some saving truths are missing.

One influential modern Protestant leader has come up with a new way to handle this dilemma. It was Protestant pastor R. C. Sproul who first famously described the Bible as a "fallible collection of infallible books."[34] Since only processes or agents (people, groups) can be fallible, Sproul is asserting that God did not protect the process by which the canon was discerned.[35] So the canon is the result of a human process that may very well have had errors—wrong books included and/ or inspired ones excluded.

Is "Reasonable" Certainty Enough?

Sproul is an internationally recognized Calvinist pastor, author, and speaker who has published numerous books and whose radio programs are broadcast worldwide. Because of his influence, many Reformed Protestants accept his statement on the canon, arguing that it's enough to know the canon with reasonable, not absolute, certainty. After all, every Christian church and denomination accepts the same New Testament; this alone is evidence that it's the true one, apart from how the conclusion was reached.

The Jews in the Old Covenant didn't have an infallible magisterium to tell them which books belonged in their canon, yet they were still the people of God and seemed to discern divine revelation just fine. So, some Protestants say, the Catholic assertion that we have to know the canon with "infallible" certainty is baseless. It is simply not necessary to have such certainty; instead, the proper use of our God-given reason can give us enough confidence in the canon of Scripture to allow us to know God's will.

BECAUSE CATHOLICISM IS TRUE,

God ensured that all Christians could have conscience-binding certainty in the canon.

Other Protestants[36] are not comfortable with Sproul's admission that the process to determine the canon was fallible. They realize that if the canon of Scripture is not inerrant, then there is no use claiming that the books themselves are inerrant. Sproul himself recognized that he had no principled reason to believe with certainty that the all too fallible Church of the early centuries correctly selected the books of the Bible, or that the likewise fallible Protestant Reformers of the sixteenth century did, either. Hence his supremely unsatisfactory formula, which has become an uncomfortable perch upon which some Protestants try to find rest from answering the question of the canon.

The main difficulty with this position is that even as it correctly identifies the problem with accepting the discernment of an "apostate" Church, or fallible reformers, or the subjective internal assessment of believers, it nonetheless accepts their conclusions in a lump. In fact, Sproul and other sympathetic Protestants believe that their Protestant canon *is* inerrant, that the list of books is exactly right, even though they flatly reject the belief that God protected from error any of the people who actually did the discernment. They are trying to produce a certainty from these various fallible sources that is somehow greater than the sum of its parts, but that is mere wishful thinking. It is not an assent of faith supported by solid reasoning but rather a fideistic leap off unstable rocks.

As for the Jews, although it's true that they did not have an infallible magisterium and that their canon grew over time as God sent more prophets to them, it's also true that the New Covenant is greater than the Old in every way. The Israelites ate manna in the desert, but the new people of God feed on Christ himself in the Eucharist. The Jews were given the Law to help them know and follow God's will, but members of the Church are given God's Spirit to help them live in the freedom of Christ. In like manner, God went beyond the Old Covenant when it came to the canon of Scripture, guiding his Church in the New Covenant to discern which books he had inspired and which he had not.

The discernment of the canon was a messy process that took centuries, during which time the Church had to sift through numerous proposed alternatives. And then, about a thousand years afterward, the Protestant Reformers came along to edit the Old Testament list of books. Sproul, one of Protestantism's foremost apologists, has taken the incredible position that though this very human-looking process was not guided by God, it somehow got the books of the Bible exactly right. I would submit that Sproul's belief is a much wilder (and less probable) article of faith than simply believing as Catholics do in a Spirit-guided Church.

THE PROTESTANT'S DILEMMA

If Protestantism is true, then the basis for all of our Christian beliefs, the Bible, may well contain books that God did not inspire, or it may leave out books that he did. At best we can be *somewhat* sure that *many* of the books of the Bible are *probably* inspired. According to the influential Protestant voice of Sproul, the canon was not infallibly selected. Therefore it may contain error. That's an unsettling thought, because if Protestantism is true, the Bible is all we've got.

11

SOLA SCRIPTURA AND CHRISTIAN UNITY

IF PROTESTANTISM IS TRUE,

Protestants should be united in their interpretations of the Bible.

Protestants hold the doctrine of *sola scriptura*: The Bible alone is the authoritative source of Christian truth. A corollary of this doctrine is the belief that the Bible's teachings are clear—at least to true Christians, whom God guides in their reading of Scripture. In theory, then, all Protestant groups that subscribe to *sola scriptura* ought to be united in belief, since they're all drawing their teachings from the one clear Scripture and are guided into truth by the same Holy Spirit. Yet Protestant churches disagree with one another on many doctrines.

Protestants Agree (Sort of)

To explain this apparent scandalous discrepancy, some Protestants insist that their beliefs are substantially similar to each other's, at least on the *important* issues: that Jesus is God, for example, and that he died for our sins and rose again. And if that is the bar for achieving unity of belief, I grant that they clear it.

But how to tell which are the "important" doctrines? Some will respond by saying "those that affect our salvation"—a reasonable place to start. Since Jesus and the apostles didn't make an explicit list of those teachings, Protestants scour the Bible (since, according the *sola scriptura,* that's where the answer has to be) for passages about salvation and strive to interpret what the inspired author is saying. Unsurprisingly, this results in conflicting conclusions even about the "essential" points of justification, sanctification, and salvation.

The Lord's Supper is a perfect example of such disagreements and how Protestants claim to resolve them. Lutherans believe that Jesus is substantially present "with" the bread and wine. Reformed Protestants believe that Jesus is spiritually present. Baptists believe that the bread and the wine are only symbolic. And some Protestants, based on their reading of Scripture, don't even celebrate the Lord's Supper.

Do these differences matter? Is the Lord's Supper an important area, one that affects salvation? When questioned about these obvious differences, some Protestants I've corresponded with have said it is, and maintained that *their* church's particular belief on this issue is correct. Others have shrugged their shoulders and said that since the relevant biblical passages can admit differing interpretations, doctrinal differences over this issue are acceptable. Some of them even say that this kind of latitude of interpretation makes for a laudable "Big Tent Christianity" that doesn't go out of its way to exclude a variety of beliefs.

In short, Protestants disagree not only on the meaning of specific doctrines but also on whether those disagreements are important or not. For some, agreeing to disagree *is* unity, the only kind of unity possible this side of heaven.

BECAUSE CATHOLICISM IS TRUE,

Sola scriptura has not led to unity but to endless divisions that show no signs of ceasing.

If, as Protestants claim, the Reformers both revived the doctrine of *sola scriptura* and restored the correct canon, *finally* basing their beliefs on the Bible alone without the taint of man-made traditions, we would expect to find perfect doctrinal unity, or at least a high level of unity, among them. Yet the historical reality is completely the opposite. Doctrinal disagreements erupted in every place Protestantism took hold: Luther's compatriot Melanchthon drifted from his more literal eucharistic beliefs; Zwingli's colleagues didn't think he went far enough fast enough in his changes to the Mass; the radical Reformers (Anabaptists) contradicted all the magisterial Reformers on infant baptism; Calvin contradicted Luther on church governance; and the Anglicans incorporated a hodge-podge of the continental Reformers' ideas into their own unique blend of Catholic-Protestant teachings, resulting in a theology abhorrent to the Puritans.

Although members of these Protestant groups all believed that they received the Holy Spirit, and were honestly doing their best to follow what they thought God was saying in Scripture, they came to different interpretations on almost every important issue. The Anabaptists, for example, rightly noticed that there was no explicit mention in the New Testament of baptizing infants, a practice that dated to the beginning of the Church and which Luther and Zwingli accepted as orthodox. That this practice was part of Christian tradition was not good enough for the Anabaptists, so they rejected infant baptism and re-baptized all Christians who joined their group (Anabaptist means "re-baptizer").

The Anabaptists did not stop there: Based on their reading of Scripture, they isolated themselves, rejecting private property on the grounds that the Bible said early Christians held everything in common. Many radical Reformers also rejected the dogma of the Trinity, arguing that it was not explicitly stated in the Bible but was a later invention of theologians. For the Anabaptists, *sola scriptura* meant relying on *no* tradition from the early centuries of Christianity (other than the tradition of the canon of Scripture, an inconsistency they apparently didn't consider). The magisterial Reformers, however, thought that the Anabaptists had gone too far; surely the Church Fathers and early councils could generally be relied upon to interpret Scripture faithfully. But who could say which side—concerning what surely must be "essential" teachings on baptism and the divine nature—was right?

Luther and Zwingli's famous dispute at Marburg[37] over the meaning of Holy Communion demonstrated that the Reformers, at any rate, did not think that differing interpretations of the Lord's Supper were insignificant or non-essential. Instead, they argued bitterly over it, refusing to admit the other's interpretation was acceptable.

Time has not smoothed over the divisions but has only brought new ones, particularly over modern issues such as same-sex marriage and women's ordination. But even the old doctrines are still subjects of dispute. The Oneness Pentecostal movement, which claims tens of millions of adherents, rejects the traditional doctrine of the Trinity, instead adopting a position close to the heresy of modalism.[38] The issues are just as essential as the ones that divided the Reformers, but just as there was no workable method of resolution then, none exists today, and the divisions increase. No honest religious historian can deny that the result of *sola scriptura* has been doctrinal chaos.

THE PROTESTANT'S DILEMMA

If Protestantism is true, then God intended for Christians to base all their beliefs on the Bible alone. The Holy Spirit would work in their hearts and minds—even overcoming the shortcomings caused by sin—to unite them in the true interpretation of the sacred text, fulfilling the perfect unity that Christ prayed for in John 17. Yet anyone who examines the array of conflicting teachings present in Protestantism from its inception until today, even in essential areas, can see that the Protestant experiment has not achieved that unity nor will ever be able to.

12

THE PRINCIPLE OF INDIVIDUAL JUDGMENT

IF PROTESTANTISM IS TRUE,

We all decide for ourselves what God's revelation means.

God inspired the books of the Bible to communicate his saving revelation to us in written form, culminating in his revelation of *himself*, in Jesus Christ. If, as Protestants believe, the Bible is the sole infallible rule of faith, God must have ensured that its meaning, at least on matters essential to salvation, would be clear to any Christian who reads it. He could not have allowed the Bible to be mysterious, obscure, or even slightly vague—even to people who weren't fluent in Greek or Hebrew. This clarity would ensure unity of doctrine among all Bible-believing Christians throughout time. As we have seen, though, such unity does not exist. This is because, in the absence of an interpreting authority, every person is left to decide Scripture's meaning for himself.

Clear Biblical Passages?

Scripture abounds with interpretative challenges. Let us consider two passages from 1 John. "If we say, 'We are without sin,' we deceive ourselves, and the truth is not in us" (1 John 1:8). A bit later we read the apostle say: "No one who remains in him [Jesus] sins; no one who sins has seen him or known him" (1 John 3:6).

An apparent contradiction exists here. From the first passage, it is clear that if we claim we don't sin, we are liars, because we do sin. But the second passage seems to say that if we remain in Jesus, we do *not* sin. What gives? Since most Protestants (along with Catholics) believe the Bible to be inerrant, this contradiction must be only an apparent one. How, then, can these two verses be reconciled?

Many Protestants who read this passage decide that in the second passage John must mean "persists in sinning" or "sins and doesn't repent." Otherwise, it would mean that if we commit a sin, which most of us do fairly often, we do not know Jesus—which sounds pretty harsh. Yet if we apply this interpretation to resolve the seeming contradiction, we are mentally interjecting new words into God's Word.

Let us consider another passage in 1 John: "As for you, the anointing that you received from him remains in you, *so that you do not need anyone to teach you*. But his anointing teaches you about everything and is true and not false" (1 John 2:27).

The simplest interpretation of this passage would be that we Christians do not need anyone to teach us, because we received the anointing from the Holy Spirit, who will teach us all we need to know. A logical deduction from this passage, combined with the ones[39] that tell us we are all priests, is that we do not need a ministerial priesthood and perhaps no type of pastor at all.

Some Quaker communities do indeed point to this passage as proof that we don't need *any* human authorities or teachers, claiming that the Holy Spirit teaches us directly. Quakers meet in services with no leader whatsoever, and only when one of the members is "moved by the Spirit" does he get up and speak a word to the others. Most Protestants do not go to that extreme and are willing to accept human authorities, at least so long as they are properly elected or display an agreeable level of spiritual knowledge. But they will still use this passage to claim for themselves a sort of "sanctified intuition,"[40] whereby their own thoughts or ideas are all of the Holy Spirit and even superior to their leaders'. Either way, the idea that we don't need anyone to teach us seems confusing, since other passages[41] in the New Testament commend us to learn from wiser elders.

When confronted with such a difficult passage, Protestants often recommend that we "use Scripture to interpret Scripture," promising that unclear or seemingly contradictory verses will be made clear or resolved by looking to other verses. This is a sensible suggestion, and indeed there are times when one passage clearly shines light on another. Perhaps this is the key to interpreting difficult biblical passages?

BECAUSE CATHOLICISM IS TRUE,

The Bible was not intended to be studied in isolation from the Apostolic Tradition and apart from the teaching authority of Christ's Church.

We just looked at a few passages that seem contradictory or unclear. (Many more could be produced easily, passages that have led to differences within Protestantism on baptism, the Eucharist, women's ordination, church structure and governance, justification, and even the Trinity.) We looked at ways that some Protestants try to resolve them. How do Catholics do it?

Regarding the first two verses, on whether Christians continue to sin or not, Catholics draw a distinction between two degrees of sin: mortal and venial.[42] Mortal sin is so grave that the Christian loses the divine life of God in his soul and thus falls from a state of sanctifying grace, putting him in peril of eternal damnation. Venial sin is of a lesser degree and does not cause the Christian to lose sanctifying grace. With this distinction, it is possible to understand John's words as meaning that no Christian who remains in Jesus continues to sin *mortally*, because to do so is to reject God in a drastic way, signaling his refusal to abide in Christ. Protestants reject that notion, believing all sin is the same, and so they must interpret the passage differently—ironically, for those professing *sola scriptura,* by imposing on it extrabiblical distinctions.

What about 1 John 2:27? Do we need anyone other than God to teach us? Catholics see this verse as needing to be understood in the context of the Church, of which John was a prominent leader. The Church of Christ is the only teacher they need—they do not need to be taught by the wicked men referenced in the previous verses, which is what John was possibly alluding to in saying they do not need teachers.

Even 1 John, which is a short and relatively uncomplicated epistle, contains many passages where the correct interpretations are not obviously clear. Throughout all of Scripture there are myriad others.

Perhaps, as some Protestants say, Scripture interprets Scripture. Maybe those who incorrectly interpret passages like those we saw above are simply failing to apply the other passages that reveal their clear meaning.

Scripture does interpret Scripture—insofar as God's revealed truth is coherent. However, using this idea as a rule for interpreting the Bible just pushes the question of interpretation back to those other verses. And it's further complicated by the question of which verses to use to interpret the problematic one. With the New Testament alone containing thousands of verses, how do we know which ones to choose? The Bible doesn't provide us with a cross-referenced index. And what if we interpret those other verses wrongly in the first place? Then we are left in the sad state of using a false interpretation to interpret another verse, which can only lead to further error.

One Protestant friend of mine belongs to a community called the Plymouth Brethren. The Brethren are dispensationalists, believing that tremendous miracles, tongues, and prophecies ceased at the end of the Apostolic Age, since the books of the New Testament had all been written by that point. They base this belief on Paul's brief statement that "as for prophecies, they will pass away; as for tongues, they will cease" (1 Cor. 13:8). The majority of other Protestant denominations interpret these verses to say that these gifts will end when Christ returns in glory, not that they ended when the last apostle died. But the Brethren are adamant about their interpretation of this passage, and it is one of their primary differentiating characteristics. Who is right? We can't ask Paul what he meant, and either interpretation could fit the text.

The founder of the Brethren, failing to see the existence of charismatic gifts, went with his gut feeling that they must have ceased and found a verse that seemed to support his instinct. And so one single verse, given a novel interpretation by someone 1,800 years after Christ, caused a further Protestant splintering and produced another new denomination.

Evangelical pastor and professor John Armstrong expressed his perplexity at the seemingly endless differences within Evangelical communities, all of which are reading the same Bible and earnestly seeking the guidance of the same Spirit:

The bigger problem was that even evangelical Protestants didn't agree with one another . . . about many important doctrines: our view of the inspiration of Scripture; how we define faith, baptism, and the Lord's Supper; church order; the doctrine of the future; the gifts of the Holy Spirit; the doctrine of the human will; and the nature of how God's grace works in salvation. The more I studied these internal evangelical debates, the longer the list grew. Something was wrong . . . but I still couldn't see exactly what it was.[43]

The problem is with the way Protestants go about trying to know divine truth. God didn't give us the Bible alone to be subjectively interpreted by every individual Christian based on his own education, reading comprehension, interests, personality, and transitory moods. Such a scheme would make each Christian his own sole authority, rather than the Church Christ founded and guided. But sadly—and unintentionally—that is where Protestantism's principles leave us.

THE PROTESTANT'S DILEMMA

If Protestantism is true, then difficult parts of Scripture should be understandable through careful study, prayerful consideration, and application of other parts of Scripture that are ostensibly clearer. Yet when faithful members of Protestant communities study hard, prayerfully seek God's illumination, and diligently apply other parts of Scripture, they still arrive at different interpretations—often leading to the founding of a new community or denomination. For a Protestant, *sola scriptura* makes him, and not the Bible, the final authority.

13

INTERPRETIVE AUTHORITY

All we have is fallible opinions about infallible books.

At the root of the endemic divisions within Protestantism lies the absence (and by definition, the impossibility) of an *interpretive authority* for Scripture above that of the individual Christian. Protestants cannot accept that any person or group has this power, because the Bible itself has to be the ultimate authority. Ideally, Protestants would be united in their interpretation of the Bible; but as we have seen, from the beginning of Protestantism this has not been the case. This lack of unity leads inevitably to the principle of private judgment, which makes each believer the final interpreter of Scripture. Just as inevitably, each believer's interpretation will be at least partly wrong, because no believer is infallible.

A Catch-22

A valid question to ask a Protestant is: How do you know that your interpretation of the Bible is correct, against the (perhaps contradictory) interpretation of any other Protestant?

The short answer is, he doesn't know for sure. And he would probably consider it dangerously cult-like to claim otherwise. But why would the Holy Spirit guide different Christians to different interpretations?

Recall that Martin Luther and Ulrich Zwingli taught conflicting interpretations of the Bible with regard to the Lord's Supper and how, exactly, Christ was "present" in the Eucharist. Luther believed that Christ was truly present in the Eucharist, while Zwingli thought his presence was figurative. Anglican scholar Alister McGrath analyzes this situation and the problem it poses for Protestantism:

> It will be obvious that these represent totally different readings of the same text. Luther's interpretation was much more traditional, Zwingli's more radical. Which was right? And which was Protestant? We see here the fundamental difficulty that the Reformation faced: the absence of any authoritative interpreter of Scripture that could give rulings on contested matters of biblical interpretation. The question was not simply whether Luther or Zwingli was right: it was whether the emerging Protestant movement possessed the means to resolve such questions of biblical interpretation. If the Bible had ultimate authority, who had the right to interpret the Bible? This was no idle question, and it lay at the heart of Protestantism's complex relationship with its core text. For this question to be answered, an authoritative rule or principle had to be proposed that stood *above* scripture—the very idea of which was ultimately anathema to Protestantism. The three leading Reformers—Luther, Zwingli, and Calvin—all recognized the importance of the question; significantly, each offered a different answer.[44]

We see from McGrath's history of the Reformation that, due to the disjointed reform movements independently springing up in different countries in the 1520s, Protestantism started out in disunity, lacking an authority that could decide whose biblical interpretation was the correct one. Not only that, but the very principles of the Protestantism made it impossible to formulate a rule that could resolve this conundrum.

The solution proposed by most Protestants is that sin or human depravity causes even Spirit-guided Christians to misunderstand God's Word. But, as we have seen, they argue that since most Protestants have come to generally similar beliefs on most important issues, the Holy Spirit has managed to create a basic consensus amid the confusion. Imagine many arrows being shot at a target. Though the archers may not have perfect aim, the Spirit corrects their shots in mid-flight and they mostly cluster around the target. We're resigned to personal interpretation, and that interpretation will be fallible, but God makes sure that together we get the big questions right in the end.

BECAUSE CATHOLICISM IS TRUE,

God wanted all Christians to know saving truth, so he has infallibly guided the Church in its teachings on faith and morals.

Not all Protestants reject the idea of an interpretive authority. Some look at the facts and recognize that it's a practical necessity. Keith Mathison, a Reformed Protestant author who penned the influential book *The Shape of Sola Scriptura*, offers a frank insight on this subject:

All appeals to Scripture are appeals to interpretations of Scripture. The only real question is: whose interpretation? People with differing interpretations of Scripture cannot set a Bible on a table and ask it to resolve their differences. In order for the Scripture to function as an authority, it must be read and interpreted by someone.[45]

Indeed, Scripture cannot be asked questions. We can't put the Bible on the witness stand and tell it to give us the whole truth and nothing but. In Protestantism, who is that "someone" who reads and interprets the Bible with authority? Mathison says it's "the Church." And "the Church" is found wherever the gospel is accurately proclaimed. But Protestants determine the meaning of the gospel through their own (fallible) personal interpretation of Scripture, creating a circular argument: The Church has authority over the individual to interpret Scripture, and you find the Church by first finding the gospel, but you find the gospel through your individual interpretation of Scripture.[46] And since all Protestants concede the fallibility of their interpretations, the whole scheme is built on thin air and must come crashing down.

Some Protestants seek to escape this dilemma by emphasizing that since the Bible is inerrant, we have a perfectly trustworthy witness. But this does not help them out of the bind, as McGrath explains:

It is perfectly possible for an inerrant text to be interpreted incorrectly. Asserting the infallibility of a text merely accentuates the importance of the interpreter of that text. Unless the interpreter is also thought of as infallible—a view that Protestantism has rejected, associating it with the Catholic views of the church or papacy—the issue of determining the "right" meaning of the Bible is not settled, or even addressed, by declaring that the sacred text is infallible.[47]

A Catholic can certainly agree that, regardless of whether an infallible interpreter exists, having an inerrant book is better than having an error-filled book. An infallible interpreter, one that can be asked questions and that can clarify its statements, is far superior—especially when dealing with passages of Scripture that produce conflicting interpretations. And that is exactly what we have in the Catholic magisterium.

Keith Mathison's belief that we should look to the Church for how to interpret Scripture is correct, but he fails to correctly identify which Church that is. He wants the magisterium, but Protestantism doesn't offer it.

Catholicism does. Christ founded the Church, established the apostles as its rightful leaders,[48] and promised to send his Spirit to guide them until his return.[49] Even in the first century we see the apostles acting with authority, interpreting Scripture and binding the faithful to their decisions.[50] Only if they had been established by divine authority would they have the right to do this; the New Testament records that they *did* have that right.[51] This same magisterium is found today in the Catholic Church, having continually exercised the authority Christ gave it. Since the Church is fully protected from error by the power and grace of God,[52] the faithful can fully assent to it, trusting that it accurately teaches God's saving truth.

THE PROTESTANT'S DILEMMA

If Protestantism is true, then no infallible interpreter of Scripture exists and thus no interpretation can be accepted as authoritative. At best we're forced to have faith that through some mysterious work of the Holy Spirit, all of our collective fallibility somehow leads us to the correct interpretation of Bible truths.

14

MISINTERPRETING THE GREAT COMMISSION

IF PROTESTANTISM IS TRUE,

Today's Protestant missionaries are misinterpreting the Great Commission.

Thousands of Protestants work as full-time missionaries in far-off lands. Yet during the time of the Reformation and for centuries after, almost no Protestants went on any missions at all! This is because the founders of Protestantism believed the Great Commission—Jesus' command to evangelize all peoples—applied only to the apostles.

No Need for Missionaries?

The Great Commission is described in the last verses of Matthew's Gospel. When Jesus is about to ascend to heaven, he gives the apostles the command to go out into all the nations to baptize and teach them. Protestants today confidently point to those verses as the biblical motivation for their missionary activities, but most of them don't realize that this interpretation is a fairly recent novelty within their ranks.

Indeed, for a few hundred years after the Reformation, Protestants understood this passage as Jesus' telling *the apostles only* to go and spread the Good News, and they believed that this work had been accomplished sufficiently in the apostolic age. The Bible was their sole rule of faith, and the Bible said nothing about the Commission extending beyond the apostles. As one historian put it:

> Both Reformed and Lutheran theologians of the last sixteenth and early seventeenth centuries, such as Theodore Beza and Johann Gerhard, argued that the Commission came to an end with the close of the apostolic age. Given this hostility toward mission within classical Protestantism, the rise of missionary activity during the eighteenth century is actually quite remarkable. . . . It was not until the 1830s that most mainline Protestant churches in the West regarded mission as a "good thing."[53]

Early Protestants believed that Christ's Second Coming was near at hand, so why set out on evangelizing missions? Further, they believed that God would take care of converting non-Christians in his own good time, basing this belief on the fact that God doesn't need any help making converts.[54]

Calvin and Luther believed that the primary "missionary" need was to reform Catholics. Calvin also argued that it was the duty of the Christian state or province—not the individual believer or even the churches themselves—to evangelize non-Christians. These beliefs strike most Protestants today as woefully erroneous, but they are consistent with Protestantism's founding principles. McGrath explains that this interpretive reversal is not surprising, given Protestantism's very nature:

> This important transition is partly explained by a classic feature of the development of Protestantism: the shifting

interpretation of core biblical texts. Definitive interpretations of those texts were offered and accepted by one generation, only to be overturned by another; a new understanding of the identity and mission of Protestantism thus
arose as being self-evidently correct.[55]

By interpreting Scripture themselves, apart from the Church's
magisterium and Sacred Tradition, the Reformers established
a novel tradition of their own that acted as a powerful influence over all Protestantism for hundreds of years. This
no-need-for-missionaries tradition colored the lens through
which other Protestants read the Bible, and only after several centuries was this tradition scrutinized and eventually dis-
carded.

BECAUSE CATHOLICISM IS TRUE,

The Church has always understood the Great Commission as applying to Christians in every era.

While the Reformers were staying home with their novel interpretation of these verses, content to poach Catholics away
from Rome, one of the greatest missionaries of all time, St.
Francis Xavier, was leaving Europe's shores for Asia to bring
the gospel to peoples who had never heard it: in Japan, Bor-
neo, and India.

This mission for Catholics to evangelize does not belong
only to the great saints. It is a call for all of us and has been
since the beginning. In the twentieth century, Pope Paul VI
reaffirmed that "the task of evangelizing all people constitutes
the essential mission of the Church."[56] He also explained,
"On all Christians therefore is laid the preeminent respon-

sibility of working to make the divine message of salvation known and accepted by all men throughout the world."[57] The history of the Catholic Church, even prior to the Reformation, demonstrates consistent commitment to spreading the gospel of Christ to the ends of the earth.

Of course, with the benefit of hindsight we know that the end of days was not imminent in the 1500s. And the idea that the state should be responsible for evangelizing seems like nonsense to us. But at the time of the Reformation, when nations and churches were deeply intertwined, this notion was much more credible. The Catholic Church, however—transcending nations, political philosophies, and time—has always known that the duty to evangelize belongs to the Church and to each of its members.

THE PROTESTANT'S DILEMMA

If Protestantism is true, either the founders of Protestantism made a huge blunder in interpreting the scriptural Great Commission, establishing a centuries-long precedent that Protestants do not go on missions, or they were right, and Protestant missionaries today are wasting their time on a pointless and unbiblical exercise.

15

THE CLOSURE OF PUBLIC REVELATION

IF PROTESTANTISM IS TRUE,

There's no reason to believe that public revelation ended with the death of the last apostle.

Virtually all Christians agree that public revelation—the "deposit of faith" given by God to man for our salvation, as opposed to private revelations given by God to individuals for some specific purpose—ended with the death of the last apostle. Because of this, we know that all necessary salvific truths have already been given to us, although we may expand or deepen our understanding of those truths over time.

Protestants believe this even though no passage in the Bible states when (or if) public revelation ended or will end. This puts them in the awkward position of affirming *sola scriptura* while also professing belief in this binding truth found nowhere in Scripture.

One Extra Revelation Needed

The popular Protestant understanding of the closure of public revelation is described in the Westminster Confession of Faith:

> The whole counsel of God concerning all things necessary for His own glory, man's salvation, faith and life, is either expressly set down in Scripture, or by good and necessary consequence may be deduced from Scripture: unto which nothing at any time is to be added, whether by new revelations of the Spirit, or traditions of men.[58]

The Westminster divines were borrowing from the long-held understanding of the Church that no more books would be inspired by God. But no biblical verses explicitly support this declaration.

Not that Protestants haven't tried to find one. Since the Book of Revelation is usually placed at the end the Bible, some of them point to Revelation 22:18[59] as evidence that no more books could be added after it. But the strongest verse that could be interpreted to support the belief that public revelation ended with the death of the last apostle is Jude 3: "I found it necessary to write appealing to you to contend for the faith which was once for all delivered to the saints." Protestants assume that the faith delivered to the saints is coextensive with the books of the Bible; so if that faith was "once for all delivered," then no more books could be inspired.

Sola scriptura therefore requires that public revelation ended. Otherwise books could be added to the Bible, and those books could contain infallible statements that would either add new truths to the existing body of revelation or, even worse, modify or outright refute Protestant interpretations of other verses. Protestants intuitively understand this principle, which explains one reason why they respond so strongly against Mormonism, which claims to be a Christian religion but has added books to Scripture.

BECAUSE CATHOLICISM IS TRUE,

Sacred Tradition also contains God's revelation to man, and it tells us when revelation ended.

The passage from the book of Revelation that warns people not to add or take away from the words of the book clearly refers only to that book (since at the time of its writing there was no single "book" of the whole Bible). Indeed, similar passages exist in Deuteronomy 4 and 12, yet, of course, many books were added to the Bible after Deuteronomy.

Jude 3 is a more interesting possibility, and in Catholic theology it is plausible to interpret the verse in a way that supports (but not proves) the belief that public revelation is closed. One problem for a Protestant seeking to use it alone as a prooftext is the probable dating of Jude itself. Unless Jude were the very last book of the Bible to be written, it makes no sense to claim that the inspired author intended his words to mean that no more books of the Bible would come after him. Scholars consider it likely that 2 Peter draws from Jude, which argues for an earlier dating of the letter, probably in the 50s or 60s. Another problem is that Jude's status as Scripture was not universally attested to—recall Luther himself appealed to this fact in his prologue to the four New Testament books he rejected, which included Jude. Since the Church took centuries to accept Jude as Scripture, it is unlikely that one of its statements would have been used to prove the closure of public revelation.

(As a side note, Jude 3 and the belief that public revelation ended with the last apostle's death also does not help us with a book like 1 Clement, written by St. Clement in all likelihood before the apostles died. Many people in the early Church accepted 1 Clement as inspired, and the letter was read in the church of Corinth and other churches for many centuries. The author was a close associate of the apostles and thus, like other books we do accept as inspired, could have written one himself.)

If this belief about the end of public revelation did not come from Scripture, where did it come from? The answer is Sacred Tradition: the revealed Christian truths that were not written down to be part of Scripture but were transmitted orally and preserved by the Church. As the Dogmatic Constitution on Divine Revelation from the Second Vatican Council explains:

> For this reason Jesus perfected revelation by fulfilling it through his whole work of making himself present and manifesting himself: through His words and deeds, His signs and wonders, but especially through His death and glorious resurrection from the dead and final sending of the Spirit of truth. Moreover He confirmed with divine testimony what revelation proclaimed, that God is with us to free us from the darkness of sin and death, and to raise us up to life eternal. The Christian dispensation, therefore, as the new and definitive covenant, will never pass away and we now await no further new public revelation before the glorious manifestation of our Lord Jesus Christ (see 1 Tim. 6:14 and Tit. 2:13).[60]

Protestants frequently attack *Catholic* truths found principally in Sacred Tradition (such as Mary's Immaculate Conception), even caricaturing the very idea of Tradition as a game of Telephone, where the original message gets garbled as it passes along a chain of people until what the last person hears doesn't even resemble the original. But they don't have a problem with accepting Tradition's judgment about the closure of public revelation, because they happen to believe that one (not to mention that guaranteeing the biblical canon is closed is also a necessary precondition for *sola scriptura*).

THE PROTESTANT'S DILEMMA

If Protestantism is true, there is no reason to say for sure that revelation is closed (since nowhere does Scripture say it is). And so the possibility remains that there may be future public revelation—like the Book of Mormon—leading to confusion and chaos among God's people.

16

THE ROLE OF HISTORY AND TRADITION

IF PROTESTANTISM IS TRUE,

Christians have zero need to understand even their own history or tradition.

According to *sola scriptura* and the principle of private judgment, Protestants believe they can discover saving Christian truth themselves, using only their Bible and the Spirit. This understanding is especially prevalent in Evangelicalism—stemming perhaps from the influence of the Radical Reformers, who were not impressed by Luther, Zwingli, and Calvin and instead took the magisterial Reformers' ideas to their logical end. As a result, most Evangelicals today know little about history and tradition, including the history of their own beliefs.

Distrust of History and Tradition

One of the events that led to the anti-traditional bent of Evangelicals was the revivalism of the First and Second Great Awakenings in the United States 200 years ago. Mark Noll, an Evangelical Protestant historian, describes this phenomenon:

The problem with revivalism for the life of the mind, however, lay precisely in its anti-traditionalism. Revivals called people to Christ as a way of escaping tradition, including traditional learning. They called upon individuals to take the step of faith for themselves. In so doing, they often led to the impression that individual believers could accept nothing from others. Everything of value in the Christian life had to come from the individual's own choice—not just personal faith but every scrap of wisdom, understanding, and conviction about the faith. This dismissal of tradition was no better illustrated than in a memorable comment by two Kentucky revivalists early in the nineteenth century. When quotations from [John] Calvin were used to argue against Robert Marshall and J. Thompson, they replied, "We are not personally acquainted with the writings of John Calvin, nor are we certain how nearly we agree with his views of divine truths; neither do we care."[61]

Even though Evangelicals owe many of their most important beliefs to John Calvin's influence, through the revival spirit of anti-traditionalism many denied any connection with him and did not even have a basic understanding of who he was. Fast-forward to today, and the situation is much the same. One Evangelical friend of mine said almost the same thing to me: "I don't care what Luther or any other Protestant teaches," much less what some Christian from the second century said—even if he was a disciple of John the Evangelist! Why don't he and other Evangelicals care what Luther or anyone else says? Because my friend has the Holy Spirit dwelling within him, and he has his Bible, so he believes from those he can individually come to know divine truth.

It is not only "Protestants in the pews" who have a low view of history and tradition. Consider well-regarded Protestant apologist William Webster, whose book *The Church of Rome at the Bar of History* sought to discredit the Catholic Church. In his section on St. Thomas Aquinas, Webster "summarizes" the *Summa Theologiae* in a mere six sentences, to the effect that Aquinas taught that faith in Jesus Christ is not vital to salvation.[62] For Evangelicals like Webster, even the most brilliant and faithful men who lived in prior centuries are superfluous to our "walk with God."

BECAUSE CATHOLICISM IS TRUE,

It's important to learn from the wisdom of those who have gone before us in faith.

One of my Anglican friends wanted to buy a book by St. Augustine, a Father of the Church who is known as the "Doctor of Grace." He happened to be close to a popular Christian chain bookstore, so he stopped in and looked around. Not finding the book, he approached the person working at the store to ask where he could find it: "Pardon me, where are your books by Augustine?" The employee looked at him blankly and responded, "Augustine who?"

This little story demonstrates an endemic problem with Evangelical Protestants: They have largely forgotten men and women who came before them in the Christian faith, those giants on whose shoulders (and prayers) they now stand. Christianity didn't end in the year 100 when the Bible was finished being written and resume again 1,500 years later when the first Baptists founded a new ecclesial community. But going into this Christian store, one is hard pressed to find a book written in the time period between the Bible and the twentieth century.

A dose of humility is the remedy. Just as we do not attempt to re-derive all mathematical and scientific formulas anew in every generation, so we should stand on the shoulders of the saintly theological giants who have gone before us. If nothing else, it stands to reason that the men and women closest in time and proximity to the apostles could give us invaluable insights into their teachings. And, indeed, this is what we see when we read their works.[63]

This is exactly the pattern followed in the Old Covenant, in which the Israelites revered and learned from the great men and women of God who had gone before them—so much so that these heroes were eulogized in the New Testament in chapter 11 of the book of Hebrews. The inspired author instructs us to learn from the examples of Abel, Enoch, Noah, Abraham, Joseph, Moses, Rahab, David, and the holy woman in 2 Maccabees 7. How much more so, then, should we learn from the great Christian saints of the past 2,000 years? Rather than reinvent the wheel (and inevitably design a worse one), we should build on the wisdom of the great men and women whom God has raised up in the Church since Christ founded it.

Even secular wisdom informs us that forgetting history condemns us to repeat it. Many of the heresies today are not new—they are unwittingly recycled from centuries past, often by well-meaning Christians who interpret the Bible apart from Tradition and the historical witness of the Church. The Catholic belief that our Lord has guided his Church into all truth through every century gives us the confidence that we can trust our forefathers in the Faith.

THE PROTESTANT'S DILEMMA

If Protestantism is true, then Christians in each generation figure out all truth for themselves, with nothing but the Bible as their guide. After all, it is quite possible that the Christians who came before us made errors, even on important doctrines, and that God is raising up new voices today to correct those errors. But how can we know which are teaching truth, and which are reviving old heresies?

17

DOING WHAT THE BIBLE SAYS

IF PROTESTANTISM IS TRUE,

Christians must follow even the seemingly absurd commands of Scripture.

Protestants point to the Bible as their sole rule of faith. But the Bible contains many commands, some of which may seem kind of strange. But they're expressed plainly enough, so they should be followed without fail. Yet Protestants don't follow them all. Instead, they use some extra-scriptural filter to help them pick and choose which ones to accept and which ones to reject.

The Word of God Says

Let's look at some biblical commands and think about whether Protestants are following them consistently. In Luke 14:12–13, Jesus says:

> When you give a dinner or a banquet, do not invite your friends or your brothers or your kinsmen or rich neighbors, lest they also invite you in return, and you be repaid.

> But when you give a feast, invite the poor, the maimed, the lame, the blind.

I cannot remember the last time that faithful Protestant friends of mine did this. In fact, I don't think any of them ever have. Yet Jesus doesn't offer any exceptions. He is quite clear that people should invite the outcasts to dinner and not their friends or relations, or wealthy people.

St. Paul is quite popular among Protestants, at least with some things he says. Less popular however are these words of his for women, in 1 Cor. 11:5–6:

> Any woman who prays or prophesies with her head unveiled dishonors her head—it is the same as if her head were shaven. For if a woman will not veil herself, then she should cut off her hair.

Although a few Protestant sects exist where women wear veils, these are a tiny minority. When was the last time you walked into a Protestant church and saw a sea of veils covering the heads of the women? This command of St. Paul's, inspired by God no less, is nearly universally ignored by Protestants.

When he speaks of marriage in Luke 16:18, our Lord says:

> Every one who divorces his wife and marries another commits adultery, and he who marries a woman divorced from her husband commits adultery.

Yet, most Protestant churches allow divorce and remarriage without any examination of the original marriage. Christ is clear here (and in Matt. 19:6) that there is no divorce and remarriage but rather only adultery when someone divorces and "marries" another. It's another tough teaching silently ignored by the vast majority of Protestant denominations.

In one of the most famous passages in the Bible, Jesus gives commands for how we are to respond when someone wrongs us. He says in Matthew 5:38–39:

> You have heard that it was said, "An eye for an eye and a tooth for a tooth." But I say to you, do not resist one who is evil. But if any one strikes you on the right cheek, turn to him the other also.

Now, most Protestants might agree that this is a good thing to do, at least in theory. But how many do it, literally or even figuratively? Very few, at best. Yet Jesus again makes no exceptions and adds no qualifiers.

BECAUSE CATHOLICISM IS TRUE,

We have a divinely ordained interpreter of Scripture to help us understand difficult passages.

It seems obvious that the Bible cannot be taken in every verse literalistically: Otherwise we'd all be breaking Christ's express command every time we throw a party with friends! A given book or passage may contain poetry, parable, apocalyptic imagery, or hyperbole, each necessitating its own interpretive principles. But the Bible itself doesn't tell us when to use *which* principle in a given instance; neither do all scholars or theologians agree on it. A Protestant, bound by *sola scriptura,* cannot appeal to a magisterium, or Sacred Tradition, or even sound principles of biblical scholarship, for all these things are extra-scriptural. When encountering difficult and even seemingly absurd scriptural data, he can only make his own interior judgment about what to accept as literal and what to interpret otherwise.

This is not a problem for the Catholic because his Church is protected from error by the Holy Spirit. He has the magisterium of the Church to guide him through.

So, for example, in the passage where Jesus exhorts his followers not to invite friends to meals, or where he commands them to turn the other cheek, the Church provides the sure interpretation[64] that in these instances Christ is teaching important principles (giving to the poor and loving our enemies are meritorious things), not giving absolute and literal moral commandments.

On the other hand, the Church teaches authoritatively that Christ's difficult-sounding words about divorce and remarriage *do* amount to a strict moral command. Likewise, that Christ meant to be taken literally when he told his followers to eat his flesh, and then at the Last Supper said, "This is my body."

St. Paul's command on head coverings for women is also instructive. Most Protestants would say that this statement was culturally conditioned; that it held for its time and a place but at some point expired. Yet nothing in the verses themselves say that or even imply it. Another principle must be brought from outside of Scripture (and therefore to the Protestant, fallible by definition) to inform the reader whether the verse should apply or not.

This is a primary cause of Protestant division: disagreement over what verses of the Bible mean, how they should be applied, whether they are essential or non-essential, and so on. One Protestant is ready to fall on his sword over women covering their heads, while another thinks it is simply obvious that that passage no longer applies to Christians. One group notices the lack of musical instruments mentioned in the New Testament and interprets it to mean that the Sunday worship service must be *a cappella*, while another thinks organs or guitars are fine.

THE PROTESTANT'S DILEMMA

If Protestantism is true, then we must obey the Bible alone, even when its commands seem impractical, even absurd, for we reject any authoritative interpreter outside of Scripture itself. Yet in practice Protestants don't do this. Instead they fill in the interpretive vacuum by silently accepting various principles and ideas that form a lens through which they read the word of God.

PART III

THE
SACRAMENTS
AND
SALVATION

18

THE COMMUNION
OF SAINTS

IF PROTESTANTISM IS TRUE,

Asking for the prayers of saints in heaven is a sort of idolatry.

Protestants agree that we can and should ask one another for prayers, but not that we should make the same request of Christians who have gone before us. (In their terminology, "the saints" refers to Christians living on earth today, not to Christians who have died in Christ and whose souls are now with God.) They base this belief on biblical prohibitions against necromancy, and on the absence of direct testimony (in their biblical books, anyway) to communion between Christians on earth and those in heaven.

Sundered Communion

Luther and the early Protestants rejected not only prayers on behalf of the dead (because they rejected belief in purgatory), but also the idea that the saints in heaven can pray for *us*. Protestants to this day likewise believe that those who have passed away, whether they are in heaven or hell, are completely disconnected from us here on Earth. This seems like common sense. Your loved one died, so that's it for any kind of relationship with him, at least until Christ returns in glory and we are resurrected. We're strictly forbidden to conjure dead spirits, and it seems no different to ask the dead for the prayers—even those who have died in Christ.

Catholic devotion to the saints offends Protestants in other ways, too: They believe only God should be honored and that venerating the saints steals glory from him; they believe that at least some Catholics turn veneration into worship and thus sin by either worshiping a person instead of God or (worse), worshiping a statue representing a person; finally the perceived macabre earthiness of relics—bones and clothes of saints, for example—evokes an almost instinctive revulsion from them. For Protestants, the dangers of Christians taking such veneration to superstitious extremes is reason enough to shun the practice, as Martin Luther described in one of his feast day sermons on the veneration of Mary:

> First Christ is diminished by those who place their hearts more upon Mary than upon Christ himself. In doing so Christ is forced into the background and completely forgotten. . . . [The monks] have used Mary as an excuse to invent all kinds of lies by which she could be used to establish their twaddle. They have used Scriptures to drag Mary by the hair and force her to go where she never intended.[65]

Luther was not against honoring Mary, but he felt that certain monks had gone too far with it, leading the people astray. Protestants today echo his fears but go still further, rejecting veneration of the saints entirely.

BECAUSE CATHOLICISM IS TRUE,

God is a loving Father who makes it possible for his children to exchange gifts with one another.

The Catholic Church teaches a doctrine called the *communion of saints*, which the Catholic Encyclopedia calls the

> spiritual solidarity which binds together the faithful on earth, the souls in purgatory, and the saints in heaven in the organic unity of the same mystical body under Christ its head. . . . The participants in that solidarity are called saints by reason of their destination [heaven] and of their partaking of the fruits of the Redemption.[66]

This ancient belief has its roots in the Bible's references to the Church being "the household of God" (see Eph. 2:19), whose members are the Christian faithful. Since we know that those who die in Christ do not die eternally but rather still live in Christ, awaiting the resurrection, the faithful who have died in God's friendship remain united to the Church, which is Christ's body (cf. Eph. 4:4–13). And so the Church as a supernatural society extends beyond those currently living on Earth. Based on these truths, since we Christians pray for one another here on Earth, we also receive graces from the prayers of the saints in heaven and can pray for the saints being purified in purgatory. Though we cannot see them, we know that they are with God and are members of his Church, as we are.

To the objection that those who have died in Christ are dead and therefore no communion with them is possible, the account of the Transfiguration poses a solid rebuttal. The great

Old Testament men, Moses and Elijah, appear before Jesus—and Peter, James, and John: "And behold, Moses and Elijah appeared to them, conversing with him" (Matt. 17:1–8). Though a Protestant might point out that Elijah had been taken up to heaven before his death, Moses certainly died (see Deut. 34). Yet Moses obviously lives, as he appears talking with Jesus in the presence of the apostles.

Couple this account of two "dead" men talking with Jesus with the revelation that Jesus used to refute the Sadducees in their denial of the resurrection: "That the dead will rise even Moses made known in the passage about the bush, when he called 'Lord' the God of Abraham, the God of Isaac, and the God of Jacob; and he is not God of the dead, but of the living, for to him all are alive" (Luke 20:37–38). Those who have passed from this world are still very much alive to God, and may even communicate with those on Earth, because God desires it and makes it possible.

The communion of saints is a spiritual family, and death cannot sunder it, because we are joined to Christ who has conquered death. So we ask our brethren here on Earth to pray for us, knowing they are in Christ, and we do the same for those who have fallen asleep in him. God is a loving Father who, like earthly fathers, delights when his children are rightly praised for the good they do in their attempts to follow his commandments.

Regarding veneration of the saints and relics, it should first be made clear that it *is* sinful for anyone to worship someone or something other than God. The Catholic Church teaches that, and if some Catholics don't know it, they need to be told. So worshiping a saint is wrong, and worshiping a statue of the saint—heaven forbid—is wrong.[67] Do we steal glory from God when we honor one of his children? On the contrary, by recognizing that the good deeds and holy lives of the saints were products of God's grace, and by seeking to emulate them, we give due honor to God.[68]

What do we make of relics? I admit that as a Protestant they repelled me. But I later realized that those feelings were caused largely by the bias that had formed within me from living in a Protestant ecclesial culture. Most Protestants don't realize that support for relics occurs even in the Old Testament, when God raised a dead man back to life through the bones of Elisha the prophet:

> And as a man was being buried, lo, a marauding band was seen and the man was cast into the grave of Eli'sha; and as soon as the man touched the bones of Eli'sha, he revived, and stood on his feet.[69]

In the book of Acts, we read that "God did extraordinary miracles by the hands of Paul, so that handkerchiefs or aprons were carried away from his body to the sick, and diseases left them and the evil spirits came out of them" (Acts 19:11–12). So whether we find relics loathsome or not, clear precedents from the inspired word of God exist for them.

The Protestant's Dilemma

If Protestantism is true, then the individualism of modern earthly Protantism also extends to those who have fallen asleep in Christ. We have no connection to those brethren who have gone to their reward in Christ, for God keeps us all separate from one another, despite the Church's being called his family. The Church's ancient practice of asking saints for intercession has all along been the grave evil of necromancy or idolatry.

19

BAPTISMAL REGENERATION

IF PROTESTANTISM IS TRUE,

The purpose and meaning of baptism are anyone's guess.

From very early on, the Church has taught the doctrine of baptismal regeneration: that through baptism people are justified and united to Christ. The Holy Spirit comes to dwell within them, and they are then said to be in a state of sanctifying grace (friendship with God). The witness of the early Christian writings is unanimous in this understanding. But Protestants today have wide-ranging, divergent beliefs about this sacrament, which spring from the conflicting teachings of the Reformers themselves.

The Protestant Spectrum on Baptism

The Swiss Reformer Ulrich Zwingli was the first major figure to propose the idea that baptism is just a symbol that signifies God's covenant with us. This novel idea was consistent with Zwingli's other theological ideas (especially the figurative interpretation of the Eucharist), and it was another point on which he diverged from Luther, who held to baptismal regeneration.

For most Protestants, especially Evangelicals, baptism is something that *they* do for *God*. It's a stand they take, a message they send to their church and to society. They make a decision to give their life to Jesus, and they get baptized to demonstrate outwardly to the church what Jesus has already done in them inwardly. They believe that God gives no grace through baptism; rather, they believe that they already received the Holy Spirit when they asked Jesus into their hearts and put their faith in him as their Lord and savior. All of the important things, the ones that Protestants believe are necessary for salvation, have thus been completed, so by getting baptized they are simply demonstrating their obedience to Jesus and making a public proclamation of their faith in him for all to see.

Luther and Calvin, on the other hand, held baptism to be more than symbolic, tying it directly to justification. Neither wished to jettison the ancient belief in baptismal regeneration. Calvin taught that baptism was the normative means of salvation, writing: "It is true that, by neglecting baptism we are excluded from salvation."[70] But Calvin *was* concerned with people believing that baptism was some kind of magical ritual. So he maintained that an obstinate person, or anyone who received it in a blind, superstitious way, would not be regenerated through baptism.[71]

Luther believed that the fundamental promise for salvation was found in Jesus' command to his apostles to baptize, found in Matthew 28. He taught, as the Catholic Church does, a sacramental understanding of baptism: that it is something that *God* does for *us*. A person places his faith in Jesus Christ, who baptized him and made promises to him through this sacrament. As *Alister McGrath put it*, "for Luther, baptism was the cause of faith"[72]—not, as for Evangelicals, merely a public sign of it. For Luther, the saving object of faith was what God has done for us through baptism.

Luther defended this belief against the Anabaptists, who claimed baptism was merely an external, symbolic act:

> But as our would-be wise, new spirits assert that faith alone saves, and that works and external things avail nothing, we answer: it is true, indeed, that nothing in us is of any avail but faith, as we shall hear still further. But these blind guides are unwilling to see this, namely, that faith must have something which it believes, that is, of which it takes hold, and upon which it stands and rests. Thus faith clings to the water, and believes that it is Baptism, in which there is pure salvation and life; not through the water (as we have sufficiently stated), but through the fact that it is embodied in the Word and institution of God, and the name of God inheres in it.[73]

Hence today Protestants see baptism as a wide range of different things: from optional memorial, to purely symbolic but important action, to an ordinance that accompanies faith, to a regenerative sacrament that causes faith to be planted.[74]

BECAUSE CATHOLICISM IS TRUE,

God regenerates us through baptism, a truth that was taught by the apostles and then transmitted without corruption to their successors.

Evidence abounds from the Church Fathers, the early Church itself, and from the Bible that baptism regenerates. Around the year 150, Justin Martyr wrote:

As many as are persuaded and believe that what we [Christians] teach and say is true, and undertake to be able to live accordingly . . . are brought by us where there is water, and are regenerated in the same manner in which we were ourselves regenerated. For, in the name of God, the Father and Lord of the universe, and of our Savior Jesus Christ, and of the Holy Spirit, they then receive the washing with water. For Christ also said, "Except you be born again, you shall not enter into the kingdom of heaven." [75]

Justin is referencing a passage from John's Gospel where Jesus is speaking to Nicodemus:

Jesus answered him, "Truly, truly, I say to you, unless one is born anew, he cannot see the kingdom of God." Nicodemus said to him, "How can a man be born when he is old? Can he enter a second time into his mother's womb and be born?" Jesus answered, "Truly, truly, I say to you, unless one is born of water and the Spirit, he cannot enter the kingdom of God" (John 3:3–5).

Justin explains that in this passage Jesus is talking about baptism. Evangelicals would say that Justin is just wrong—that being "born of water" means one's *natural* birth. So, to be saved, you must be naturally born and then born again by the Spirit (through a conversion experience). However, apart from being a little nonsensical (why would Jesus mention natural birth as a prerequisite for salvation?), this interpretation is directly contradicted by all the many Church Fathers who wrote about baptism.[76]

Baptism is also explicitly mentioned in the Nicene Creed: "We confess one baptism for the forgiveness of sins." Interestingly, this creed is affirmed not only by Catholics and Orthodox but also by most Protestant communities. Yet Protestants do not believe that God forgives sins through baptism! So Protestant Christians are left in the inconsistent position of affirming this ancient creed while making a mental exclusion for the words "one baptism for the forgiveness of sins," interpreting them to mean something like "one baptism for the symbolic, outward proclamation that one has put his faith in Jesus."

Scripture contains many passages supporting baptismal regeneration. One of the clearest is from 1 Peter 3:20–21:

> [W]hen the patience of God kept waiting in the days of Noah, during the construction of the ark, in which a few, that is, eight persons, were brought safely through the water. And corresponding to that, baptism now saves you not the removal of dirt from the flesh, but an appeal to God for a good conscience through the resurrection of Jesus Christ.

Just as God saved Noah and his family through the ark, Christ gives us new life through baptism, which cleanses us from sin and thus gives us a "good conscience."

On the day of Pentecost, Peter exhorts the people to receive baptism: "Repent, and each of you be baptized in the name of Jesus Christ for the forgiveness of your sins and you will receive the gift of the Holy Spirit" (Acts 2:38). Protestants like to emphasize the "repent" part at the negation of the "be baptized" part, but both are essential. Paul, too, later in Acts, reinforces baptism's essential role when he says: "Now why do you delay? Get up and be baptized, and wash away your sins, calling on his name" (Acts 22:16).

Because Protestants have been immersed in a tradition that rejects baptismal regeneration, when you show these verses to them you can almost see the scales falling off their eyes. They wonder how they never realized that Scripture connects baptism with forgiveness of sins and spiritual rebirth.

THE PROTESTANT'S DILEMMA

If Protestantism is true, then the early Church—along with Luther and Calvin—was wrong to teach the doctrine of baptismal regeneration, and the formulation "one baptism for the forgiveness of sins" in the Nicene Creed means something other than what the plain words suggest. Or perhaps the opposite is correct. Further, this interpretation of biblical verses suggesting baptismal regeneration is mistaken, leading to a skewed and misplaced emphasis on the importance of baptism over faith. Or maybe it's right. The one thing Protestantism can say for sure is that Christ commanded his disciples to baptize the nations because baptism is essential for salvation. Unless it isn't.

20

INFANT BAPTISM

IF PROTESTANTISM IS TRUE,

We don't know for sure whether infants should be baptized—not only dividing churches but potentially imperiling millions of souls.

Should infants be baptized? That simple question split the movements within Protestantism from the beginning and continues to be a divisive issue among them. The unchanging teaching and practice of the Catholic Church, based on Scripture and Tradition, is to baptize infants. Protestants all look to the Bible alone as the sole infallible rule of faith, yet one group comes to the conclusion that baptizing infants is laudable, while the other condemns the practice.

The Protestant Movements and Tradition

The Anabaptists (literally, "rebaptizers") were the radical movement within the Reformation. They rebaptized anyone who followed them because they rejected infant baptism as invalid, claiming that the Bible taught credo-baptism ("believer's baptism"). To them, *sola scriptura* meant that every doctrine should be explicitly found in the Bible without the influence of traditions, even those of the early Church as found in the writings of the councils, the Fathers, and other early Christians. If a doctrine was not explicitly stated in the Bible, then it was not to be taught as true, and they rightly pointed out that nowhere in the New Testament does it explicitly say that an infant should be baptized.

If their theological innovations ended there, perhaps some accord could have been reached between them and the other reforming movements. The Anabaptists went further, however, and asserted that the doctrines of the Trinity and of the divinity of Christ were also not explicitly found in Scripture and thus should not be accepted. These incredible claims were based on the belief that the Bible could be accurately interpreted by any Christian who had the Holy Spirit and that an individual's judgment could trump that of the Church.

The magisterial Reformers—Luther, Zwingli, and Calvin—were appalled by the radical Reformers' rejection of such fundamental Christian teachings. For them, it was good and even necessary to look to the traditions of the early Church and to the writings of the Fathers—especially those of Augustine—in order to formulate true doctrines. The magisterial Reformers believed that these past Christians had (for the most part) developed sound biblical theology by correctly interpreting Scripture. Any errors they saw in the Fathers' teachings would of course be corrected by their own, wiser understanding of theology, but the core doctrines were to be preserved insofar as they were in harmony with the Bible. And the Trinity, the divinity of Christ, and infant baptism were most certainly in harmony with the Bible.

Protestantism today has inherited this centuries-old division from its founding fathers. (The situation is even more dizzying, given the vast number of denominational splits that have occurred since the 1500s.) Most Protestant traditions practice infant baptism, but large groups of Protestants—especially Baptists, most other Evangelical Protestants, and the very populous Pentecostal communities—reject it as unbiblical.

BECAUSE CATHOLICISM IS TRUE,

Infant baptism is consistent with revealed truths in Scripture and Tradition. Moreover, infants should receive baptism, because through it God infuses in them sanctifying grace, which saves.

Although no biblical verses command or explicitly describe infant baptism, various passages provide strong evidence that babies and small children received the sacrament. For example, recall Peter's testimony to the crowds at Pentecost: "Repent, and be baptized, every one of you, in the name of Jesus Christ for the forgiveness of your sins; and you shall receive the gift of the Holy Spirit. For the promise is to you and to your children" (Acts 2:38–39). Here he makes no mention to exclude children who had not yet reached the age of reason. Elsewhere in the New Testament (Acts 16:33, 1 Cor. 1:16) we read about entire households being baptized, and these would have included servants, children, and infants.

The Church Fathers also witness to infant baptism. In the early 200s, Hippolytus wrote: "Baptize first the children, and if they can speak for themselves let them do so. Otherwise, let their parents or other relatives speak for them."[77] And later that century, Cyprian of Carthage, in a council with many other bishops, defended the practice:

As to what pertains to the case of infants: You [Fidus] said that they ought not to be baptized within the second or third day after their birth, that the old law of circumcision must be taken into consideration, and that you did not think that one should be baptized and sanctified within the eighth day after his birth. In our council it seemed to us far otherwise. No one agreed to the course which you thought should be taken. Rather, we all judge that the mercy and grace of God ought to be denied to no man born.[78]

Later in the same letter, Cyprian reaffirms in no uncertain terms that infants, even ones just born, should be baptized without hesitation.[79] Many other Church Fathers similarly testify to infant baptism's being a noble and ancient teaching of the Church.

Martin Luther's beliefs on infant baptism and the reasons for it were likewise quite Catholic. Recall that Luther believed God communicated grace to the person being baptized, and that it was God himself who baptized through the minister. Luther also recognized that the Church had always baptized infants, up to and including the sixteenth century when he began the Reformation. Combining this universal practice of the Church with his sacramental understanding of baptism, "Luther regarded infant baptism as the means by which God brought about faith in individuals."[80]

In other words, God bestowed the theological virtue of faith on the individual through the sacrament of baptism. Luther offered an eminently reasonable explanation of how we can know that infant baptism is pleasing to God:

But if God did not accept the baptism of infants, he would not give the Holy Ghost nor any of his gifts to any of them; in short, during this long time unto this day no man upon earth could have been a Christian. Now, since God confirms Baptism by the gifts of his Holy Ghost as is plainly perceptible in some of the church fathers, as St. Bernard . . . and others, who were baptized in infancy, and since the holy Christian Church cannot perish until the end of the world, they must acknowledge that such infant baptism is pleasing to God.[81]

His reasoning is compelling: If infant baptism is invalid, then the vast majority of Christians (who were baptized as infants) were invalidly baptized, and thus never received the Holy Spirit or the virtues of faith, hope, and love. They were therefore not members of Christ's Church and thus could not even be rightfully called Christians. On the other hand, if infant baptism is valid, then the Protestant groups practicing credo-baptism were denying children the supernatural help they needed to be saved.

Either the magisterial Reformers were correct in teaching infant baptism even though it's not explicitly mentioned in Scripture, or the radical Reformers were correct in rejecting infant baptism as an unbiblical practice on which the Church had fallen into error from the beginning. To accept the radical Reformers' interpretation, as most Evangelicals do, would concede to them a credible claim to faithful scriptural interpretation—tough to do, given the Anabaptists' rejection of the Trinity and Christ's divinity, with which only a tiny minority of modern Protestants would agree. On the other hand, to side with the magisterial Reformers also raises a thorny question: If we accept this particular tradition of the early Church, even though it isn't explicitly defined in the Bible, on what basis do we reject other ancient traditions such as prayers for the dead, the Mass, purgatory, the primacy of the church of Rome, and baptismal regeneration—all of which have as much as or even more scriptural support than does infant baptism?

THE PROTESTANT'S DILEMMA

If Protestantism is true, we would expect that a subject as important as who should and who shouldn't receive baptism would be clear from Scripture. But it manifestly is not, and faithful Protestants have fallen on different sides of the issue for almost 500 years. In the balance hang the millions of souls who as infants were either baptized invalidly or denied baptism's saving grace.

21

SANCTIFICATION AND PURGATORY

IF PROTESTANTISM IS TRUE,

When we die, God waves a magic sanctification wand over us wretched, filthy sinners to make us suddenly fit for heaven.

Psalm 24 asks, "Who shall ascend the hill of the LORD? And who shall stand in his holy place?" The psalmist immediately answers: "He who has clean hands and a pure heart." Similarly, Jesus tells his listeners in Matthew 5:8, "Blessed are the pure in heart, for they shall see God." Purity of heart is a requirement to be able to "see God." Yet Protestantism maintains that even justified Christians are impure in their hearts, their sanctifying works defiled.

Christians Remain Impure in Heart

Protestants believe that salvation consists of two main parts: justification and sanctification. For them, justification is that one-time event in which the unregenerate man accepts Jesus as Lord and Savior and has Christ's righteousness imputed to him. His sins are forgiven; he is now a Christian. Sanctification now begins.

This sanctification is an ongoing process whereby the Holy Spirit gives grace to the believer and helps him follow God's will (see Ephesians 2:10) in order to become more like Jesus. So far, so good. But these works and this grace do not make the Christian truly pure in heart, nor are the works themselves pure and holy. As the Westminster Larger Catechism says in question 78:

> The imperfection of sanctification in believers arises from the remnants of sin abiding in every part of them, and the perpetual lustings of the flesh against the spirit; whereby they are often foiled with temptations, and fall into many sins, are hindered in all their spiritual services, and their best works are imperfect and defiled in the sight of God.

Note that even "their best works" are "defiled in the sight of God," because it is impossible for the believer, even with the help of God's grace, to obey God perfectly. Jesus may have said that we must be perfect like the Father,[82] but Protestants deny that this is possible.

Further, we cannot even become pure in heart, for "the remnants of sin" abide in "every part" of us. Our hearts remain defiled, and the works they produce are tainted. Even the most minor of the "many sins" that the Christian falls into on a daily basis are not negligible, for "there is no sin so small, but that it deserves damnation."[83] All this stems from the root Protestant doctrine of justification—that we are not truly made holy in justification, only declared so. The image of the Christian as a dung mound covered in snow, distilled from Martin Luther's writings, remains an apt description of how Protestants believe that Christians remain impure, in spite of God's grace.

And if we are impure, then we cannot see God, as both the Old Testament and Jesus testify that we cannot appear before God unless we are pure in heart.

BECAUSE CATHOLICISM IS TRUE,

Through sanctification we are truly made holy, empowered by the Spirit to fulfill the New Covenant law of love.

The Catholic Church teaches that justification is not just a divine legal fiction wherein the Christian is declared to be something he is not (righteous). Instead, by grace through faith united to God's love, God inwardly justifies the Christian by the power of his mercy, infusing his sanctifying grace into him, making him pure of heart. The tendency to sin, it is true, is still there. The Church calls this *concupiscence*. But its existence does not render null or tainted the good works that Christians do in God's grace. The *Catechism of the Catholic Church* says, "With justification, faith, hope, and charity are poured into our hearts, and obedience to the divine will is granted us."[84]

This makes the Protestant conception of sanctification look self-contradictory and empty, as Jason Stellman, a long-time Presbyterian pastor turned Catholic convert, pointedly expressed:

> While sanctification is insisted upon in the Reformed [Protestant] paradigm, the fact that not a single thing we do in this life is deserving of anything but hell, together with the fact that all one's future sins are forgiven in justification, brings me to the conclusion I stated above: In the Reformed system, sanctification is a mere footnote to justifi-

cation, an optional afterthought that consigns our Spirit-wrought works of love and sacrifice to the level of mere response that, while great if it's actually offered, doesn't have any causal relation to our being saved in the end.[85]

In Catholicism, sanctification is not an afterthought but the process whereby we become holy, so that when our earthly life comes to an end, we are prepared to meet God with a clean heart. This paradigm, which maintains that we can truly become holy by God's grace, harmonizes with the Bible better than does the Protestant paradigm. St. Paul writes in Romans:

> For just as you once yielded your members to impurity and to greater and greater iniquity, so now yield your members to righteousness for sanctification. . . . But now that you have been set free from sin and have become slaves of God, the return you get is sanctification and its end, eternal life.[86]

The end of sanctification is eternal life. But what if the justified Christian fails to become fully sanctified in this life? Simple, he goes to purgatory after death. There the process of sanctification will be completed, his heart purified so that it is fit to see God. All the attachment to sin and selfishness, as well as the temporal punishment due for sin, are purged in the cleansing power of God's love. The choice for the Christian is clear: either be sanctified in this life, through meritorious works and prayerful endurance of the sufferings and reverses that come your way, or do so in the next life through suffering alone.

This comports perfectly with the difficult passage in St. Paul's first letter to the Corinthians:

Now if any one builds on the foundation with gold, silver, precious stones, wood, hay, straw—each man's work will become manifest; for the Day will disclose it, because it will be revealed with fire, and the fire will test what sort of work each one has done. If the work which any man has built on the foundation survives, he will receive a reward. If any man's work is burned up, he will suffer loss, though he himself will be saved, but only as through fire.[87]

Purgatory is that state after death in which Christians are being saved through proverbial fire. Since Protestants reject this doctrine, and further since they reject the biblical teaching that we can fulfill the law of love by God's grace, the only way they can enter God's presence is by his waving the magic wand of sanctification over them at death, so that their impure hearts will be automatically purified, rendering them fit for seeing God.

THE PROTESTANT'S DILEMMA

If Protestantism is true, then neither Jesus' command to be holy nor the grace he offers us to become so have any real meaning. We should also expect to find in the Bible many references to the powerlessness of God's grace to make us pure in heart, as well as explicit testimony to the instant holiness (waving of the sanctification wand) Jesus grants us right before we walk through heaven's gate. Instead, Jesus and the apostles tell us we can *truly* become holy and pure in heart, by God's grace, and we can do works that are fitting and holy.

22

MARRIAGE
AS A SACRAMENT

IF PROTESTANTISM IS TRUE,

Marriage is not an outward sign of an inward grace wrought by God, even though Protestants sometimes act like it is.

The Catholic Church teaches that "sacraments are outward signs of inward grace, instituted by Christ for our sanctification."[88] We have seen that Protestants, following the lead of Martin Luther, explicitly rejected five of the seven sacraments, including marriage. Confusingly, however, most Protestants effectively *do* believe that marriage is an outward sign of inward grace, in unwitting rejection of their founding theology.

Marriage: A Secular Contract or Covenant

In rejecting the Catholic sacramental theology of marriage, Luther placed it squarely in the earthly, as opposed to heavenly, kingdom. But while he considered it nothing more than a contract, enforced by the civil authorities, he believed that God used it for divine purposes, so it was not without spiritual value. Calvin went further and, later in his life, developed a theology and legal framework for marriage based on his belief that marriage was a covenant between the spouses and God. He wrote:

> God is the founder of marriage. When a marriage takes place between a man and a woman, God presides and requires a mutual pledge from both. Hence Solomon, in Proverbs 2:17, calls marriage the covenant of God, for it is superior to all human contracts. So also Malachi declares that God is as it were the stipulator who by his authority joins the man to the woman, and sanctions the alliance.[89]

We see that, although Calvin stopped short of calling marriage a sacrament, he attributed a covenantal status to it and believed that God was its author.

Anglican Protestantism also viewed marriage as divine in origin, even while denying that it was a sacrament. Reading the words of the traditional Anglican wedding ceremony, it's difficult to find anything that differs from Catholic theology:

> Dearly beloved, we are gathered together here in the sight of God, and in the face of this congregation, to join together this Man and this Woman in holy Matrimony; which is an honourable estate, instituted of God in the time of man's innocency, signifying unto us the mystical union that is betwixt Christ and his Church; which holy estate Christ adorned and beautified with his presence, and first miracle that he wrought, in Cana of Galilee. . . . [God], knitting them together, didst teach that it should never be lawful to put asunder those whom thou by Matrimony hadst made one.[90]

Notice the admission that marriage resulted in the union of the two persons. They became one—an inward grace if there ever were one—through the outward signs of the wedding ceremony, the vows, and the consummation. This Anglican ceremony even recognizes, as Catholics do, that Christ elevated marriage through his participation and miracle-working at the wedding in Cana.

Protestants today esteem marriage highly, recognizing its goodness and its analogy to Christ's marriage with his bride the Church. Following Calvin, most view it as a covenant between the husband, the wife, and God, though one that can be dissolved for a wide variety of reasons.

And therein lies the rub. It's a dissoluble union, not a sacrament. In the Old Covenant, we learned that Moses let them divorce due to the hardness of their hearts,[91] and for Protestants not much has changed since then: divorce for any reason and remarriage at will. So although they would *like* marriage to have some deep, spiritual, quasi-sacramental aspect—and historically they attempted to claim such an aspect—by rejecting its sacramental indissolubility, they forfeit any claim to such an interpretation. For Protestants, the New Covenant essentially makes no difference when it comes to marriage, even though they pay lip service to what Christ said and did about it.

BECAUSE CATHOLICISM IS TRUE,

We know that Christian marriage is a sacrament, a sign of God's grace ordered toward salvation.

Genesis 2:24 says, "That is why a man leaves his father and mother and clings to his wife, and the two of them become one flesh." In Mark 10, Jesus reaffirms this teaching on marriage in explaining why divorce is impossible. From these verses and the universal witness of Christian history, clearly marriage is something instituted by God and pleasing to him. A Christian man and woman have a wedding ceremony where they exchange marriage vows. Then they consummate their vows through the marital embrace, and *in doing so, they become one flesh*. God joins them together as one, and even if they were to separate or to have their civil marriage dissolved, in God's eyes—and therefore in reality—they are still married. Thus, the sacrament of marriage is an *outward sign*—through the wedding ceremony, the dress, the rings, the bells, the procession, the vows, the marital embrace—that signifies the inward grace that unites the couple as one flesh.

Catholics thus enjoy the integrity of treating marriage like a sacrament *and* believing it to be one. Thus the Church recognizes that a valid marriage between baptized persons is *indissoluble*. If there is a civil divorce, the spouses may not marry someone else while the other is still alive—it would be an impossibility. For God has joined them together, and man cannot sunder them. Protestant churches, on the other hand, marry divorced Christians all the time. Lacking the theological commitment to marriage as a sacrament, they believe that various actions by either spouse can break the covenant between them.

THE PROTESTANT'S DILEMMA

If Protestantism is true, marriage should not be considered a sacrament, a visible sign by which God bestows invisible grace on a couple to make them one flesh. This despite the desire of most Christians, following biblical teaching, to believe that marriage has at least a quasi-sacramental character—though not when it comes to divorce and remarriage.

23

ANOINTING
OF THE SICK

IF PROTESTANTISM IS TRUE,

The anointing of the sick is not a sacrament, even though the Bible attests to it in multiple places.

In the anointing of the sick, a priest or bishop anoints the sick person with blessed oil and prays over him for the Holy Spirit to heal his body and soul. Although it is rooted in Scripture, the Reformers ended this practice, curiously giving different reasons for the decision.

The End of the Anointing

Martin Luther argued that since people who received it during his day were typically on their deathbed, and most did not recover from their illness, it could not be a true sacrament. (If it were, he reasoned, God would heal every person who received it.) As we have seen, he also rejected the book of James (in which can be found some scriptural support for the sacrament) as uninspired, and even when he assumed for the sake of argument that James was canonical, he nonetheless believed that an apostle had no right to "create" a sacrament.

He also claimed that the Gospels make no mention of it.

John Calvin followed Luther in rejecting this sacrament, though he gave a different reason for doing so: he believed that God no longer worked miracles through his ministers.

> But the gift of healing disappeared with the other miraculous powers which the Lord was pleased to give for a time, that it might render the new preaching of the gospel for ever wonderful. Therefore, even were we to grant that anointing was a sacrament of those powers which were then administered by the hands of the apostles, it pertains not to us, to whom no such powers have been committed.[92]

This type of theory falls into a theological category called dispensationalism, which divides up history into different periods, or dispensations, to try to explain why God has seemingly worked in different ways over the course of the centuries.

The vast majority of Protestant churches today do not practice the anointing of the sick. They reason that, because the Bible does not record Christ explicitly commanding its usage as he did for baptism and the Eucharist, anointing cannot be a sacrament and is at best an optional practice that a church could choose to do.

BECAUSE CATHOLICISM IS TRUE,

Anointing of the sick was instituted by Christ, practiced by the apostles, and intended to continue as a sacrament of God's grace throughout the history of the Church.

Martin Luther made an error in assuming that the person's physical recovery was the vital component of the anointing he received. Instead, the sacrament is meant first for the *spiritual* health of the person, especially for those persons who were soon to meet God (note Christ's priorities toward the seriously ill in Matthew 9:2–7). In claiming that the Gospels don't mention the sacrament, he ignored or embarrassingly missed Mark 6:13, where the Jesus sends the apostles out, and they anoint with oil to heal sick people.

We see clear evidence elsewhere in Scripture of the apostles administering the sacrament. For example, James 5:14–15: "Is anyone among you sick? He should summon the presbyters of the church, and they should pray over him and anoint (him) with oil in the name of the Lord, and the prayer of faith will save the sick person, and the Lord will raise him up. If he has committed any sins, he will be forgiven." The biblical witness and the historical practice of the Church from the earliest centuries in both East and West confirm that this sacrament was apostolic and instituted by Christ. Yet the Protestant Reformers rejected it, and all of Protestantism followed after them.[93]

St. John Chrysostom, the eloquent Doctor of the Church, confirmed the importance of the sacrament and its connection to the role of the priesthood in the forgiveness of sins:

> The priests of Judaism had power to cleanse the body from leprosy—or rather, not to cleanse it at all, but to declare a person as having been cleansed. . . . Our priests have received the power not of treating with the leprosy of the body, but with spiritual uncleanness; not of declaring cleansed, but of actually cleansing. . . . Priests accomplish this not only by teaching and admonishing, but also by the help of prayer. Not only at the time of our regeneration

[in baptism], but even afterward, they have the authority to forgive sins: "Is there anyone among you sick? Let him call in the priests of the church, and let them pray over him, anointing him with oil in the name of the Lord. And the prayer of faith shall save the sick man, and the Lord shall raise him up, and if he has committed sins, he shall be forgiven."[94]

Calvin's dispensational theory is almost without anything to recommend it. It is arbitrary, without foundation either in Scripture or Tradition. It is startling that one of the most influential men behind Protestantism could so cavalierly dismiss one of the seven sacraments of the Church using only his own made-up theory to do so. And yet his opinion has continued to influence Protestant theology even down to our day.

When I was an Evangelical Protestant going to a Southern Baptist church, my pastor gave a sermon in which he recounted his experience of being asked by a hospitalized church member to come and pray over him and anoint him with oil. The church member explicitly mentioned James 5 as the biblical precedent for the request. My pastor said, "Sure enough, I looked it up, and it's right there in the Bible just like he said. So I didn't really know what to do, but I went to the hospital and took some oil with me, and then, well, *I poped him!*"

This last statement was accompanied by the pastor making the gesture of the sign of the Cross. Raucous laughter and applause from the congregation followed. (I might have found it funny, too, had I not recently begun to consider that the Catholic Church's claims might be true and therefore that this sacrament being joked about might in fact be something ordained by God.) This Baptist church claims the Bible alone as the sole source of revelation and rule of faith, yet my pastor had never done what James said, right in the Bible, that he should do.

THE PROTESTANT'S DILEMMA

If Protestantism is true, then anointing of the sick is not a sacrament. Catholic and Orthodox Christians have been smearing oil on sick people's heads for centuries in futility, erroneously believing the biblical passages that say it will forgive their sins.

24

THE EUCHARIST

IF PROTESTANTISM IS TRUE,

Christ may be present somehow in the Eucharist, or it may be a purely symbolic and even optional ritual. Or it may be a demonic form of idolatry.

Infant baptism is one polarizing issue for Protestantism. The Eucharist is another. What did Jesus mean by, "This is my body?" Catholics (and Orthodox) believe that he really meant it, and that the bread and wine become his real body and blood. Protestants took a wide range of divergent positions on it, the only commonality among them being the condemnation of what the Catholics believed. Although some Protestant beliefs on the Eucharist—such as traditional Lutheranism—are relatively close to that of Catholicism, most others hold to a purely symbolic understanding and look aghast upon Catholics who prostrate themselves before a piece of bread.

Is This My Body?

Luther took Jesus at his word, but he rejected the philosophical underpinnings of the Catholic dogma of transubstantiation in favor of something called sacramental union, the idea that Jesus is present *with* or *beside* the bread and wine. Zwingli, the Swiss Reformer, broke from the Catholic Church and from Luther by declaring the equally novel idea that the Eucharist merely *signifies* Christ's body. Calvin, as usual, tried to steer a path in between his two predecessors.

Luther and Zwingli met early on in their respective reformations to try to come to an agreement on the Eucharist, but neither would budge. They utterly failed to agree, to compromise, or even to find common ground on which to move forward with discussions. Luther trenchantly observed that if, when Jesus said "This is my body," he didn't in some real way *mean* "This is my body," then it is impossible for anyone to accurately interpret the scriptures. Since Luther taught the doctrine of the perspicuity of Scripture, the error couldn't be that the Bible was not clear but that others (such as Zwingli) interpreted its clear words wrongly.

John Calvin believed that the Lord's Supper was more than just a symbol, yet he differentiated himself from Luther by coming up with his own interpretation of our Lord's words and their meaning:

> We begin now to enter on the question so much debated, both anciently and at the present time—how we are to understand the words in which the bread is called the body of Christ, and the wine his blood. This may be disposed of without much difficulty, if we carefully observe the principle which I lately laid down, viz., that all the benefit which we should seek in the Supper is annihilated if Jesus Christ be not there given to us as the substance and foundation of all. That being fixed, we will confess, without doubt, that to deny that a true communication of Jesus Christ is presented to us in the Supper, is to render this holy sacrament frivolous and useless—an execrable blasphemy unfit to be listened to.[95]

Calvin stressed that Christ communicates himself to us through the Eucharist, earlier in this same treatise asserting that, in the sacrament, "the Lord displays to us all the treasures of his spiritual grace."[96] But, lest an unwary reader think Calvin was sympathetic to Catholic Eucharistic theology, the Reformer went on to denounce in polemical terms the doctrines of transubstantiation and the sacrifice of the Mass.[97] Calvin rejected in no uncertain terms the Catholic dogma of the Real Presence.

The situation today in Protestantism is no clearer. The spiritual descendants of each of the Reformers generally hold to the position of their forefather. Lutherans and Anglicans hold a weekly service that is liturgical and always includes a celebration of the Lord's Supper. The Eucharist for them is more than a symbol (while remaining less than the Catholic doctrine of the Real Presence). Presbyterians and Reformed Protestants, following Calvin, hold to his covenantal view of the Lord's Supper, which again is more than a mere symbol, but different from the Lutheran notion of sacramental union.

But the majority of Protestants belong to the Evangelical, non-denominational, or Pentecostal strains and so believe that the Lord's Supper is simply a memorial and nothing more (though, it should be said, nothing less). Theologian Craig Blaising enunciates the Evangelical position on the Lord's Supper well:

Historically, Baptists have reacted to sacramental views of grace which they argue are not biblical. Baptists believe that Zwingli was basically correct in seeing a metaphorical intent in the Lord's remarks at the Last Supper. . . . Baptists see no justification in Scripture for connecting grace to anything other than the direct gift of God to personal faith directed to his Word of promise. There is no doubt that a sacramental view of the Eucharist did develop through the early centuries of the Church so that a Real Presence view *came to be found within* church teaching. But Baptists do not believe this was in fact the view of the New Testament churches.[98]

Blaising believes that the Real Presence was a heretical teaching that arose within the Church along with many others. But unlike other heresies that were rightly condemned, the Real Presence became instead enshrined as the orthodox belief. Although Blaising does not go so far as to call Catholics bread-worshipers, some Evangelical Protestants[99] do take that step. From their perspective, the communion matter does not become Christ's body and blood, so Catholics kneeling down before mere matter and adoring it as if it were Jesus is a most disgusting form of idolatry.

BECAUSE CATHOLICISM IS TRUE,

Christ is really present in the Eucharist, just as he said.

"This is my body." Jesus could not have been any clearer; and yet, to the Reformers and to Protestants after them, it evidently wasn't clear enough. Rather than re-treading ground well covered by other Catholic apologists regarding Scripture and the Eucharist,[100] I would like to offer a brief explanation of the biblical passage that tipped the scales in my own mind on the Real Presence.

In John 6, the Bread of Life discourse, Jesus explains that he is the living bread that came down from heaven, bread that a man can eat and live forever. Up until verse 51, a purely figurative interpretation of his words seems possible. "Believing in Jesus" is the work he wants us to do,[101] so eating his flesh must simply be another way of saying, albeit in a strange way, that we have to believe in him. But from verse 53 to 54 and onward, in answer to the confusion expressed by the Jews at his words, Jesus does something very odd (if Protestantism is true, and the Eucharist is figurative): He makes the eating of his flesh even *more* graphic by using a different word[102] for eating, rendered as the Greek *trogo,* denoting an animal-like gnawing. In the subsequent verses, he doubles down on this more primal way of eating by continuing to use *trogo*:

> He who eats my flesh and drinks my blood has eternal life, and I will raise him up at the last day. For my flesh is food indeed, and my blood is drink indeed. He who eats my flesh and drinks my blood abides in me, and I in him. As the living Father sent me, and I live because of the Father, so he who eats me will live because of me. This is the bread which came down from heaven, not such as the fathers ate and died; he who eats this bread will live forever.[103]

Jesus must have known that his listeners would rebel at these words, given God's injunction in the Old Covenant against consuming blood.[104] And his followers did what he must have expected them to do: They left *en masse*. So much so that he turned to the Twelve, as if they were the only ones who remained, and asked if they, too, would abandon him over this teaching. If he had been using a mere figure of speech, he would have consoled his disciples by telling them so. It would have made no sense to drive them away by leading them to believe something that he did not mean.[105] And so the ancient Church's teaching on the Real Presence of Christ in the Eucharist harmonizes perfectly with the Bread of Life discourse; Protestantism's dissenting opinions on it do not.

Reading the Church Fathers and other early Christians, Zwingli's purely symbolic notion of the Eucharist (shared by most Evangelicals today) is nowhere to be found. Instead we find widespread profession of the Catholic dogma of the Real Presence. Luther certainly knew this fact, being well-versed in early Christian writings, which is no doubt one reason why his teaching of sacramental union was, at least on paper, very close to the Catholic Church's understanding of the Eucharist.

Take Ignatius of Antioch, for example, who lived during the apostolic age and died in the first decade of the 100s. He wrote against the Docetist heretics, who taught that Jesus only *appeared* to be a truly flesh-and-blood human being:

> Take note of those who hold heterodox opinions on the grace of Jesus Christ which has come to us, and see how contrary their opinions are to the mind of God. . . . They abstain from the Eucharist and from prayer because they do not confess that the Eucharist is the flesh of our Savior Jesus Christ, flesh which suffered for our sins and which that Father, in his goodness, raised up again. They who deny the gift of God are perishing in their disputes.[106]

In the second and third centuries, Justin Martyr, Irenaeus, Clement of Alexandria, Tertullian, Hippolytus, Origen, and Cyprian of Carthage likewise all attested to the Real Presence of Christ in the Eucharist.

Perhaps no other doctrine presents as decisive a litmus test as does the Eucharist: Either the Church for fifteen centuries was right, or one of the Reformers was. Each Reformer confidently presented his own opinion as divine truth, with Calvin even claiming that the question "may be disposed of without much difficulty." Really? Humility would suggest extreme caution to anyone who chose to contradict the Church's universal teaching on such an essential issue, yet instead we get Calvin's cavalier brashness. Luther likewise presented his innovation as patently true, and Zwingli as well.

Christ's words indicate that eating his flesh and drinking his blood is a matter directly concerning one's salvation—it's not an area where wide theological speculation is acceptable. Yet in Protestantism today the beliefs range all over, a multi-headed Hydra of private judgment that leaves honest inquirers bewildered as to what they should believe about it. No certainty can be found here except through individual bosom-burning, and such subjective feelings are too ephemeral to be trustworthy, especially with salvation at stake. The only universal commonality among the various Protestant Eucharistic theologies is the inexorable conclusion that, in believing Christ is really present in the Eucharist, Catholics are idolaters who worship bread and wine. And since the early Church taught this same Catholic doctrine early on, Christians for untold centuries were idolaters as well.

THE PROTESTANT'S DILEMMA

If Protestantism is true, the Church has demonstrated, once again, that its beliefs were corrupted from early on and that it cannot be trusted to teach the truth on any matter of faith. For over a thousand years, nearly all Christians bowed in worship before mere bread and wine, wrongly thinking Jesus was there. Only in the 1500s was the true teaching on the Eucharist recovered. But who can say whether that true teaching belonged to Luther, Zwingli, or Calvin?

25

CONFESSION

IF PROTESTANTISM IS TRUE,

The power that Jesus gave men to forgive sins died with the apostles.

For Protestants, it seems clear from the New Testament that God forgives sin directly, without agents or intermediaries. The whole point of Jesus' becoming man, after all, was to reveal to us that we now had direct access to God. Matthew's Gospel describes the temple veil being torn in two at Christ's death, demonstrating that the separation between man and God was now overcome. Further, nowhere in the Bible is there an explicit description of the Catholic confession ritual. Sacramental confession may have been an ancient practice, but this was simply another corruption in the early Church.

Sacrament Retained, Sacrament Discarded

At first, Luther actually retained the sacrament of confession, along with the Eucharist and baptism. But since it depended on an ordained clergy, and one of Luther's key points was the rejection of any distinction between clergy and laity, he ultimately decided that the sacrament had to go. The rest of Protestantism, as it had done on so many other fundamental doctrines, followed his lead.

Perhaps above all others, this sacrament incenses Protestants, who believe that since only God forgives sin, going to a mere human being to receive forgiveness is unbiblical. True, John 20:21–23 seems to support it:

> (Jesus) said to them again, "Peace be with you. As the Father has sent me, so I send you." And when he had said this, he breathed on them and said to them, "Receive the Holy Spirit. Whose sins you forgive are forgiven them, and whose sins you retain are retained."

But many Protestants interpret this passage as saying that when *we proclaim the gospel to people* we are in effect declaring that their sins are forgiven (if they accept it) or declaring that God has not forgiven them (if they reject it). Similarly, to them the passages where Jesus gives the apostles authority to "bind and loose" (Matt. 16:19, 18:18) are about declaring what God has already decided in heaven. Thus God does not use people as agents for forgiving sins; rather we're just messengers of the forgiveness that God grants.

Other Protestants find that interpretation to be a stretch and claim that God *did* use the apostles as instruments of forgiveness of sins but that this ability was given only to the apostles. When the last one died, the power of forgiveness died with him. (This is another dispensational theory, like Calvin's rejection of anointing of the sick).

BECAUSE CATHOLICISM IS TRUE,

God chooses to work through man, to share the gospel, to be his hands and feet, and even to forgive sins.

In the sacrament of confession, the repentant Christian confesses his sins to a priest, and the priest, acting with Christ's divine authority, forgives him and reconciles him to Christ's Church (which he wounded by his sin). It must be understood aright that it is God who forgives sins, but, as he does in so many other ways, God chooses to communicate his grace through human instruments. Scripture indeed teaches that only God can forgive sin; on this Catholics agree with Protestants. But Scripture also teaches that he shares this divine authority with his chosen human ministers.

Protestant interpretations of John 20:21–23, although not completely outside the realm of possibility, are not the most straightforward way to understand the passage. What if it simply means what it clearly says, and nothing more or less? The Bible says that Jesus gave his apostles the power to forgive sins, and neither Scripture nor common sense leads us to conclude that this power disappeared in the first century.

Unsurprisingly, this is exactly how the early Christians seemed to understand it. St. Ambrose wrote in the 300s about confession and the power God gives to priests to forgive (or not forgive) sins in his name:

> Consider, too, the point that he who has received the Holy Ghost has also received the power of forgiving and of retaining sin. For thus it is written: Receive the Holy Spirit: whosesoever sins you forgive, they are forgiven unto them, and whosesoever sins you retain, they are retained. . . . The office of the priest is a gift of the Holy Spirit, and his right it is specially to forgive and to retain sins.[107]

Hippolytus, Tertullian, Origen, and many other early Christians confirmed the practice of sacramental confession to a priest.

It must be noted that this is God's *ordinary* means of bestowing the grace of forgiveness. A Protestant who wholeheartedly and humbly confesses his sins as he has been taught to confess (which varies greatly within Protestantism) doesn't necessarily miss out on forgiveness. God is never bound by his own designs. At the very least, though, the Protestant does miss out on the peace that Catholics enjoy as they leave the confessional with the freedom of knowing that they have been forgiven.

Catholics can agree that the temple veil's being torn in two does demonstrate that, through Christ, we now have direct access to God. In no way can this be construed to mean, however, that God then quit using men as instruments of salvation. If anything, Christ's Incarnation suggests the opposite. God chose to save us through a man, the God-Man, providing us a supreme example of human cooperation with divine grace.

Finally, we should recognize that sacramental confession does not rule out confessing our sins privately to God as well. Catholics can and do directly pray to God daily and have a relationship with him, but this relationship is not just about "me and Jesus." It involves the Body of Christ, the Church, and it honors Jesus' decision to work through people to administer grace.

THE PROTESTANT'S DILEMMA

If Protestantism is true, even though the Bible says Jesus gave men the power to forgive sins, and the early Church exercised this power, the sacrament of confession was an evil perversion only done away with in the sixteenth century when the Protestant Reformers rejected it. Christians for 1,500 years lived under the delusion that when they confessed their sins to a priest, they were truly forgiven by God, when in reality they were placing their trust in a false human tradition that imperiled countless millions of souls.

26

HOLY ORDERS AND APOSTOLIC SUCCESSION

IF PROTESTANTISM IS TRUE,

Anyone who accurately interprets and teaches from the Bible has authority in Christ's Church.

The Catholic Church teaches that a validly ordained priest or bishop is necessary for the administration of several of the sacraments: anointing of the sick, the Eucharist, confirmation, confession, and holy orders—the sacrament by which a man becomes a deacon, priest, or bishop. But although the early Church believed that holy orders transmitted authority from the apostles to their successors, Protestants assume that at some point this line of authority was corrupted and broken. The Reformers, in recovering the true, biblical gospel of Jesus, received authority to proclaim the truth, and so do all Bible-believing Protestants to this day.

Apostolicity=Authority

Martin Luther rejected the distinction between clergy and laity under the banner of "the priesthood of all believers," and so he rejected the sacrament of holy orders. In doing so, he also rejected the doctrine that Christ's divine authority is transmitted through apostolic succession. Recognizing this foundational doctrine, the Catholic Church teaches that it takes a validly ordained bishop to ordain another bishop. But how did the ordaining bishop get ordained? From another validly ordained bishop, following a line that goes back to the apostles themselves, who were ordained by Jesus Christ. This authority was then transmitted to the apostles' successors, as it was to Matthias (who replaced Judas in Acts 1:26) and the first bishops (such as Timothy in 1 Timothy 4:14). The direct line of authority continues to the current bishops today of the Catholic Church (as well as the Orthodox churches, which have kept the succession unbroken).

Luther knew that he had to reject apostolic succession; otherwise he could not justify causing a schism from the Church and establishing another church based on his own authority. At the same time he needed plausible justification for that authority. So he and the other Reformers posited a new idea: that authority is given by God to whoever teaches the true gospel—a doctrine sometimes called *apostolicity*.[108] This broke the Catholic Church's monopoly on apostolic authority and opened up that authority to Luther, Calvin, the Anabaptists— to anyone, really, who thought that he was teaching the truth from the Bible.

The Reformers were appalled by the behavior of Catholic clergy, some of whom were corrupt and worldly. They also thought that Catholics had twisted the gospel beyond recognition. We can understand why they rejected the idea that Catholic bishops retained rightful authority in Christ's Church. Christ *must* have revoked authority from them long ago, when corruptions began to pollute the true gospel. Protestants today use this same reasoning today to reject the teaching that apostolic succession is the means by which divine authority was transmitted to the leaders of the Church.

Christ gave divine authority to the apostles, and they in turn to their successors, continuing one bishop to another down through the ages.

Which idea is right: apostolic succession or apostolicity? Let's consider a few passages from early Christians, beginning with one from Augustine, the great Church Father respected by Catholics and Reformers alike:

> For if the lineal succession of bishops is to be taken into account, with how much more certainty and benefit to the Church do we reckon back till we reach Peter himself, to whom, as bearing in a figure the whole Church, the Lord said: "Upon this rock will I build my Church, and the gates of hell shall not prevail against it!" The successor of Peter was Linus, and his successors in unbroken continuity were these: Clement, Anacletus, Evaristus, Alexander, Sixtus . . . Damasus, and Siricius, whose successor is the present Bishop Anastasius.[109]

Clement, the close successor to Peter himself, wrote within the first century:

> The apostles have preached the gospel to us from the Lord Jesus Christ; Jesus Christ [has done so] from God. Christ therefore was sent forth by God, and the apostles by Christ. Both these appointments, then, were made in an orderly

way, according to the will of God. . . . And thus preaching through countries and cities, they appointed the first fruits [of their labors], having first proved them by the Spirit, to be bishops and deacons of those who should afterwards believe. Nor was this any new thing, since indeed many ages before it was written concerning bishops and deacons. For thus says the Scripture in a certain place, "I will appoint their bishops in righteousness, and their deacons in faith." Our apostles also knew, through our Lord Jesus Christ, that there would be strife on account of the office of the episcopate. For this reason, therefore, inasmuch as they had obtained a perfect foreknowledge of this, they appointed those [ministers] already mentioned, and afterwards gave instructions, that when these should fall asleep, other approved men should succeed them in their ministry.[110]

These are only two examples of the many writings of the early Christians attesting to apostolic succession and the ministerial priesthood. Prior to the Reformation, the Protestant notion of apostolicity was a foreign concept. But since Protestants do not have valid succession from the apostles, they must reject holy orders as the sacrament by which divine authority is transmitted to men, by Christ, through other ordained men.

The lack of holy orders and apostolic succession creates a vacuum of authority in Protestantism. Enter apostolicity to fill it, as a necessary corollary to *sola scriptura*. The Bible alone is the sole infallible rule of faith, and no person or group of people is protected from error by God in interpreting Scripture, so every Protestant is his own ultimate interpretive authority. Naturally, he thinks his interpretation of Scripture is substantially correct, and he follows those Protestant pastors and scholars who agree with his interpretation. These men and women, he reasons, must be the ones with authority, because they are teaching God's truth to others. And he himself also has this authority because he shows others how his interpretation of the Bible is true.

Joseph Cardinal Ratzinger, now Pope Emeritus Benedict XVI, offers a striking contrast between God's work of apostolic succession and the self-appointment that is at the heart of apostolicity:

> This is precisely what we mean when we call ordination of priests a sacrament: ordination is not about the development of one's own powers and gifts. It is not the appointment of a man as a functionary because he is especially good at it, or because it suits him ... it is not a question of a job in which someone secures his own livelihood by his own abilities, perhaps in order to rise later to something better. Sacrament means: I give what I myself cannot give; I do something that is not my work; I am on a mission and have become the bearer of that which another has committed to my charge. Consequently, it is also impossible for anyone to declare himself a priest or for a community to make someone a priest by its own *fiat*. One can receive what is God's only from the sacrament, by entering into the mission that makes me the messenger and instrument of another.[111]

Protestant communities view their ministers, who are "ordained" by the fiat of the community and not through a sacrament, as functionaries rather than as persons specially configured to Christ through holy orders. This flawed conception represents a fundamental misunderstanding of the way that God instituted rightful authority in his Church.

What of the idea that clerical immorality was a sign that God had withdrawn authority from the Church? Well, the leaders of God's Church have always been sinners. Some have followed Christ more faithfully than others, but none has been perfect. So it's impossible to support the claim that sinful bishops must have lost their authority. The apostles themselves would have been excluded by such a criterion!

The charge that they lost authority when they began teaching a corrupted gospel seems to have more merit. But this just begs the question. For who, exactly, has the authority from God to discern the true gospel from a corrupted one? Who can correctly interpret the data of divine revelation? And how would the rest of us know?

THE PROTESTANT'S DILEMMA

If Protestantism is true, any man or woman intelligent and faithful enough to correctly interpret Scripture has authority from God. But Protestants judge their pastors' interpretations of the Bible against their own interpretation, which may very well be erroneous, so they can never be sure of who has true authority in the Church. Catholics can know who has rightful authority based on the orderly succession of bishops, from the early Church down through today.

PART IV

CHRISTIAN HISTORY AND PRACTICE

27

SEXUAL MORALITY

Sexual morality is culturally conditioned and thus subject to change.

All Christian churches once recognized homosexual behavior as a sinful aberration. Today, many Protestant groups not only accept such behavior as normal, they endorse (even conduct) same-sex marriages. This is just the latest domino to fall—after contraception and premarital sex—in the collapse of traditional Protestant sexual morality, which has become ever more compromised by the spirit of the age.

A Sea Change in Protestantism

The Evangelical Lutheran Church in America (ELCA) is the largest set of Lutheran communities in the United States with more than four million members. In 2009, the members of the ELCA voted to endorse clergy who are in homosexual relationships, opening "the ministry of the church to gay and lesbian pastors and other professional workers living in committed relationships."[112] In doing so, they realized they were overturning centuries of Bible-based Christian moral teaching, but they believed that Jesus wants them to do so, as a matter of justice and equality for all people. The ELCA was following in the footsteps of the Episcopal Church, which had ordained an open homosexual as bishop in 2003, and which adopted a resolution in 2009 to allow individual bishops to decide whether to bless same-sex unions, and would three years later designate an official liturgy for such blessings. With civil law throughout the Western world rapidly redefining marriage to include same-sex couples, many other Protestant groups have followed suit or are in a period of evolution.[113]

This evolution logically follows from another historical change: Protestantism's acceptance of contraception. Beginning with the Anglican Communion in the early twentieth century,[114] nearly all of Protestantism has come to embrace the idea that marriage is about sex and companionship first, procreation second. Once marriage and babies were so divorced, Protestants had no principled objection to unions of same-sex couples, who could argue that they offer each other the exact same kind of partnership that heterosexuals do.

It is not just on contraception that Protestants have waffled. Even historically conservative Evangelicals are turning away from longstanding Christian opposition to fornication. In a recent survey, an astounding 80 percent of Evangelicals ages 18 to 29 claimed to have engaged in premarital sex, and a large majority were sexually active in the past year.[115] This reality has prompted many Protestant leaders to take the incredible step of encouraging these unmarried Christians to use contraceptives when they have premarital sex.[116]

Mark Driscoll, a hugely popular Protestant mega-church pastor, wrote a sermon series on contraception (including sterilization). His statements typify the common Protestant attitude—including from conservative Evangelicals—toward these issues. He writes that methods such as "condoms . . . the diaphragm, contraceptive sponges, cervical caps, and female condoms," in addition to sterilization procedures, "are options for Christian couples to consider." In defending his position, he writes:

> [T]here are Christians who are legalistic on this issue and declare that there is essentially never a good reason for such a permanent measure. However, life in a fallen world is complicated and painful. For example, a pastor and his wife who are good friends of mine suffered eighteen miscarriages before he had a vasectomy to stop what had become for them incredible physical and emotional pain.[117]

While my wife and I can sympathize with his friend who has suffered numerous miscarriages, citing the "fallen world" and its complexity is not sufficient to justify actions contrary to the Bible and the Church's Tradition.

BECAUSE CATHOLICISM IS TRUE,

Sexual morality transcends time and the shifting sands of cultural opinion.

Interpreted accurately, the Bible supports the traditional norms for sexual morality. St. Paul says in 1 Corinthians that "neither the immoral, nor idolaters, nor adulterers, nor sexual perverts . . . will inherit the kingdom of God."[118] Jesus tells his listeners that even looking lustfully at a woman in one's heart, let alone committing physical adultery with her—is evil. And for hundreds of years, Protestants agreed with the Catholic interpretation of these verses. That has changed.

Examining the history of contraception and same-sex acts shows us that Christians universally rejected them as immoral. Contraception was condemned by all churches and ecclesial communities until 1930. No Christian church recognized the morality of homosexual relationships or the validity of same-sex "marriages" until recent years. Premarital sex is still officially taught to be immoral by most Protestant churches, but clearly the young people in those churches aren't receiving the message.

These radical reversals in Protestantism's beliefs on sexual morality stem from a rejection of the natural law and their embrace of nominalism: They reject the idea that humans can recognize the nature of things, that the body has inherent meaning because it reflects the person.[119] Even Protestant pastors fall to this error, because, following Protestantism's bedrock principle of *sola scriptura* and individual interpretive authority, they choose to believe that only those practices that a Christian interprets to be explicitly condemned by the Bible are off limits. Everything else is fair game if both parties *consent* to it.

Because they hold to *sola scriptura*, Protestants can look only to the Bible itself for binding arguments for or against same-sex relationships. Though some Protestants claim to recognize Christian "tradition," what happens in practice is that these Protestants pick and choose in an *ad hoc* way from Tradition when it suits them (for example, opposing homosexual acts) but reject that same Tradition when it does not (contraception, premarital sex, and so on). These examples provide strong evidence that the Bible was never intended to be an exhaustive manual for faith and morals.

Catholics, on the other hand, draw from Scripture *and* the Apostolic Tradition, building upon the natural law, to know truth in its fullness. The natural law can get us as far as heterosexual marriage, and Scripture and Tradition, as interpreted authoritatively by the Church's magisterium, can reveal to us the full beauty and splendor of God's design. The husband and wife make a total gift of themselves to each other, becoming a communion of life and love that images the communion between the divine persons of the Holy Trinity. Within the total, lifelong commitment of marriage, children find the ideal environment to learn to love.

Let's analyze why certain sexual acts are immoral. Though at first glance they may seem unrelated, same-sex acts and contracepted sex both disconnect sexual pleasure from openness to life, to procreation. The sexual act should be one of mutual love that unites the husband and the wife and that is open to the gift of children:

> Finally, this [married] love is fecund. It is not confined wholly to the loving interchange of husband and wife; it also contrives to go beyond this to bring new life into being. "Marriage and conjugal love are by their nature ordained toward the procreation and education of children. Children are really the supreme gift of marriage and contribute in the highest degree to their parents' welfare."[120]

This fecundity is what makes the marital act self-giving. Homosexual acts and contraception are intrinsically selfish and closed in on themselves, for they can never be life-giving. And having sex before marriage risks the possibility of conceiving a child, a child who would not be given a true family structure that she deserves.

Catholics can argue in the public square, even without using Scripture, by appealing to natural law, the law written on our hearts by God himself. We can offer principled objections to same-sex "marriage," but in doing so we also point out to our Protestant brethren that contraception and premarital sex are against our nature and against divine law. Protestantism in recent times has not only shown the failure of *sola scriptura* to uphold sexual morality but in fact has deployed arguments from (biblical) silence against Catholics and others who still hold the line against these evils.

THE PROTESTANT'S DILEMMA

If Protestantism is true, then traditional Christian standards of sexual morality have either been wrong for two millennia or they can change with the times. If they've been wrong, what other teachings could be wrong? And if they can change, what else can change?

28

OTHER MORAL ISSUES

IF PROTESTANTISM IS TRUE,

Christian moral teachings are subject to change based on a majority vote.

For hundreds of years, Protestantism stood firmly with traditional Christian orthodoxy on all issues of morality. But in the past century, many Protestant denominations have altered (in some cases, reversed) their teachings not just on sex but also on other important moral subjects such as abortion and the indissolubility of marriage. As with sexual morality, these Protestants have employed a democratic model for discerning Christian teaching, implying that Christ's moral teachings can change with the spirit of the age.

Protestant Reversal on Abortion and Divorce

From the Reformation until the 1960s, all Protestant groups condemned abortion as evil, but as the winds of modern society began to shift, so did Protestant teachings. It began with the Episcopal Church in 1967, when its General Convention voted to approve abortions in certain situations.[121] The dominoes continued to fall over the next five years, with the Presbyterian Church USA (PCUSA) reversing its pro-life position to support unrestricted access to abortion, the Lutheran

Church in America (a precursor to the Evangelical Lutheran Church in America (ELCA) declaring it was the decision of the woman, and the United Methodists, the United Church of Christ, the Disciples of Christ, and even the Southern Baptist Convention following suit.[122]

Some Protestants even use the Bible in an attempt to prove that life does not begin at conception. One verse used to argue for when life begins, even by Evangelicals, is Leviticus 17:11: "For the life of the flesh is in the blood." Since it takes weeks after conception for the baby to pump blood, an argument is made that abortion before this time is acceptable.

Other Protestants go further and argue from the Bible that life does not begin until breath is drawn:

> Many people think that a human being is created at the time of conception but this belief is not supported by the bible. According to the bible, a fetus is not a living person with a soul until after drawing its first breath. After God formed man in Genesis 2:7, He "breathed into his nostrils the breath of life and it was then that the man became a living being." Although the man was fully formed by God in all respects, he was not a living being until after taking his first breath.[123]

I don't find this logic compelling, for several reasons, but the Bible does contain verses that *could* be construed as supporting the notion that life begins weeks or even months after conception.

All of Christianity likewise once considered marriage to be an indissoluble bond, but today most Protestant communities have reversed their past teachings and permit their members to divorce and remarry. Tellingly, the first Protestants laid the shaky foundation for undermining marriage, beginning with Martin Luther and King Henry VIII. Luther was a Catholic priest, which means he had "married" the Church. Yet he broke in schism from her and then chose to marry a nun who had herself broken her vows (religious sisters are seen as being spiritually "married" to Christ). King Henry VIII drove the Church in England into schism over the desire to divorce his wife and marry another. In the well-known but tragic story that is the start of the Anglican Church, Henry VIII had two of his subsequent wives executed and divorced another.

Still, Protestantism maintained a strong respect for marriage, following the broader Christian society's opinion. But as society changed, so did Protestantism. Without the strong foundation that marriage was an inviolable sacrament, Protestants were primed to be led astray by the spirit of the age. And so they were.

Modern wisdom views personal fulfillment as the highest good. We are encouraged to "follow our bliss," do what's "good for *us*," and recognize that sometimes people "fall out of love." When a marital relationship is no longer gratifying, divorce is seen as an acceptable and even necessary course. Secular ideologues warn us that it's unhealthy to keep a lifelong promise when we no longer feel fulfilled by it.

Without the supernatural protection of the Holy Spirit, Protestant denominations simply have no defense against the creeping tide of secularism that the world has embraced. Protestants see abortion and divorce as, at best, necessary evils in the quest for one's self-actualization, and at worst, handy tools for extricating oneself out of a tough situation. They've swallowed the modernist heresies that place the individual on a pedestal above all else.

BECAUSE CATHOLICISM IS TRUE,

The Church's moral teachings were true yesterday, today, and forever.

The Catholic Church stands today virtually alone in recognizing the immorality of contraception and sterilization. Similarly, the Church continues its unchanging witness to the sanctity of human life from conception to natural death by condemning abortion unequivocally.

One does not need to understand or accept the Church's authority to agree with this condemnation, of course. There are many Protestants who remain pro-life on biblical grounds. In fact, even basic arguments from biology and natural law suffice to establish the immorality and injustice of abortion.

The question of divorce and remarriage, however, is less obvious. When the Protestant Reformers threw out most of the seven sacraments, they fundamentally damaged the theology behind marriage: the understanding of marriage's nature and goods. This has unsurprisingly led to modern Protestantism's almost univocal approval of divorce and remarriage.

The Catholic Church, on the other hand, has retained the theology of marriage it received from Christ and the apostles: that a true marriage between baptized persons is sacramental and indissoluble (Matt. 19:8–9). That is why it continues to preach the same hard but loving truth that Christ taught: for validly married persons to divorce and marry someone else is to commit adultery.[124]

Of course, sometimes Catholics do obtain a civil divorce and then enter Christian marriage with someone else. They're able to do this because, due to the presence of some obstacle or defect at the time of the first attempted marriage, a valid union was never formed. When petitioned to determine whether such an obstacle actually existed, rendering invalid the attempt at marriage, the Church undertakes a serious and thorough legal investigation called the process of annulment. If this process determines that a true marriage never occurred—that the man and woman never actually became one flesh in God's eyes—both persons are free to enter into marriage with someone else.

Annulments are not "divorce Catholic-style." Unlike divorce, which requires a marriage to have existed, annulments require that a marriage *never* existed. The circumstances that could impede a marriage from occurring, though they're beyond the scope of this book to discuss in detail, are not trivial. Also, marriages are never annulled due to "irreconcilable differences," infidelity, or any other factor that arose after the wedding.

Our world, so deeply in need of a Christian witness to the sanctity and permanence of marriage, instead sees the rampant divorce and remarriage among Christians as proof that these evils are acceptable, and that God doesn't seem to help Christians stay married any more than other people. This weakening of marriage has led to the disintegration of the family, which is the fundamental cell of society. Along with contraception, which removed the necessity of children from marriage, it has paved the way for the rise of acceptance of same-sex unions and "marriages."

It is no coincidence that the Catholic Church has stood like a rock, unmoved and unchanged in its moral teachings against the battering waves of the modern world with its selfish and morally relative agenda. The bishops, priests, and laity of the Catholic Church have not accomplished this feat by their own strength but by the unfailing protection of God's Spirit.

THE PROTESTANT'S DILEMMA

If Protestantism is true, then not even the sanctity of human life can be considered non-negotiable Christian teaching. Along with the indissolubility of marriage, it's not an objective moral truth but a mere starting point for negotiation with the secular culture.

29

THE DISINTEGRATION
OF MAINLINE
PROTESTANTISM

IF PROTESTANTISM IS TRUE,

**There's nothing wrong with choosing
a church based on your tastes and
interests rather than God's truth.**

On a recent trip to the grocery store, I saw two bumper stickers for churches: the Powerhouse Church and the Cactus Cowboy Church. I have a friend who goes to a very hip, artsy Protestant church called Mosaic, which denies that it is a "church" in the standard sense. Neither of these churches falls into traditional categories, nor are they affiliated with a standard denomination. The mainline Protestant denominations are shrinking rapidly, leading some to predict a coming collapse of Evangelicalism,[125] so it is not surprising to see the rise of such "niche" churches. We are all looking for community, and more than ever Protestants are choosing one-off congregations that most "fit" them and their personal preferences.

Ecclesial Consumerism

Ask a young adult who goes to a denominational church how he would describe himself and you will likely hear, "I am a Christian; I go to this church because they teach soundly from the Bible." He would not label himself a "Baptist" or a "Methodist." Denominational loyalty doesn't bind him as it did his parents, back when families often formed religiously homogenous communities. Irish theologian Alister McGrath talks about this fading denominational loyalty within Protestantism: "Even as late as 1960, most Americans had serious misgivings about worshiping at Protestant denominations other than their own, feeling this compromised their religious identities. Their loyalty was primarily—and in many cases exclusively—to the specific beliefs, structure, and life of a particular denomination."[126]

If what really matters is believing in Jesus and following him, not where you go to church, then people will choose a church based on where they feel "fed" and able to contribute their own gifts. Of course a cowboy is going to love it at the Cowboy Church, where there's a barbecue after every Sunday service and the elder rides a horse.

Just as I have my unique taste in coffee—mint mocha latte, decaf, whip—if I can have a church that fits my exact tastes, that's where I'm going. If I don't fit into the categories of Anglican or Churches of Christ or Pentecostal, I can go instead to where I have found a community that relates to my personal journey with Jesus.

This mentality fits into our Western culture's consumeristic idea that we should have multiple choices for everything. Why should I go to a church that "I don't get anything out of?" I don't willingly subject myself to inconvenience and pain in other areas of my life, so why do it on Sundays? I want a church that fits my tastes, plays worship music I like, has people of the same age and demographic as me, provides activities that I find meaningful, and teaches articles of faith and morals that make me feel good about what I already believe and do.

BECAUSE CATHOLICISM IS TRUE,

The Church that Christ established and has guided into all truth can still be found today.

At the heart of Protestantism's ecclesial consumerism is an assumption that there is no one true, visible Church that we all need to reunite with; instead, all churches are small parts of the invisible Church, each offering something unique. So choosing one over the other is like choosing a different dish at a restaurant.

The Catholic understanding is the opposite. There *is* a visible Church that Christ established, but Protestant communities have broken off in schism from it. Choosing a church is therefore nothing like choosing a kitchen appliance or an espresso, and the focus should never be on what works for "me." Instead we try to conform ourselves to what God has ordained.

And so our search should not be for the church that fits our personal preferences but for the Church that Christ built and to which he appointed rightful authorities, the Church that he promised to protect from error and lead into all truth, the Church that the gates of hell cannot prevail against.[127] Certainly, *within* that Church will be people grouped by different interests and callings—there is legitimate diversity within the unity of the truth (1 Cor. 12:12–27). But on Sundays, we should all kneel united before the cross of Christ, recite the one creed, and offer the same sacrifice. Christ called us to unity (John 17:21), so he must desire it *and* make it possible for all types of people to achieve.

THE PROTESTANT'S DILEMMA

If Protestantism is true, then no one Church has the fullness of the truth; rather, all churches teach a mixture of true and false doctrine. So it makes sense to find one that agrees on enough of the truth that you deem essential and also that appeals to your tastes and preferences. In addition, as your tastes change and your church feels less relevant, it's your right to find a different church that meets your needs. In the end, this makes being a follower of Christ more about us than about him.

30

PASTORAL AUTHORITY

IF PROTESTANTISM IS TRUE,

**You never know which leaders,
if any, have true authority.**

I once listened to a series of talks given by an Evangelical pastor, whom I will call Pastor Neil, which focused on equipping men to be faithful and strong disciples of Christ. One important point he made was the idea of *jurisdiction*, which, in Pastor Neil's parlance, was equivalent to *authority*. He rightly pointed out that men, as heads of our families, have authority given to us by God the Father and that we must accept this authority and use it to lead our families in a Christ-like way. *In a similar way, he said,* rightful Christian authorities should lead those in their churches. That makes sense, too. But how to figure out who exactly *has* that authority is much less clear.

I Have No Authority but Jesus

We all have human authorities in our lives. At home when we were children, our parents were our authorities; at school, our teachers and principals were. In civil society, we have authorities at many levels: city council, mayor, law enforcement officers, legislators. We see that they have authority over us when we break the laws they enact and enforce—because we get a ticket or go to jail! At work, too, we have authorities over us; I have no fewer than six levels of supervisors above me in the authority chain that goes right up to the top of my company.

But what about in the Christian faith? Ah, here it is different, is it not? Here, surely, we have "no authority over us except Jesus Christ," which is exactly what many Protestants say when it comes to their beliefs and their church. According to Protestant theology, Jesus is the only infallible authority, so it is only to him that a Christian can give his unqualified allegiance.

Yet we know that in the Bible God also revealed offices of Christian leadership: elders, presbyters, and deacons. And so within Protestantism a tension exists between God's ultimate authority and the subordinate authority held by the human beings Scripture says should be in charge of local churches. When a Protestant believes there's a conflict between what his elders are telling him and what he understands God's will to be, he must follow the latter—even if it means breaking off and starting his own church. Does an elder still retain authority if he falls into error? Each Protestant answers that question for himself, judging his leaders based on his own interpretation of what God's authority says in Scripture.

The consequence of this is clear: If a leader's authority is only as good as his followers' judgment of his leadership, then he never had true authority to begin with. Once again, private interpretation reigns supreme.

BECAUSE CATHOLICISM IS TRUE,

God guides the rightful authority of his Church, so submitting to its authorities is submitting to God.

Here's what Pastor Neil had to say about authority: "Pride will destroy a jurisdiction. Don't trust Mohammed or Buddha: Who gave them jurisdiction? Why should I listen to one of them? They don't have jurisdiction. Where men do not submit to their elders, there will be destruction and disorder in the church. If a man won't listen to the elders, to the church, if he won't submit to their jurisdiction, Paul says, 'I will deliver such a one to Satan' and his jurisdiction [1 Cor. 5:4–5]." Pastor Neil also mentions that Peter told Christians to submit to the government, superiors in the work sphere, human institutions, and authorities for the Lord's sake.

What if we were to apply Pastor Neil's ideas to the beginnings of Protestantism? Martin Luther and the other leaders of the Reformation did not submit to their elders, the bishops of Christ's Church, and that did indeed lead to "destruction and disorder." It led to schism upon schism, to a thousand splinterings that countermanded Christ's command, and Paul's, that there be no divisions among Christians.

"If a man won't listen to the elders, to the church, if he won't submit to their jurisdiction, Paul says, 'I will deliver such a one to Satan' and his jurisdiction." How many times has this happened in Christ's Church through history? The Manichees, the Monophysites, the Docetists, the Arians, and many other men who chose to reject the elders of Christ's Church and their authority were delivered to Satan and his authority. So why exactly did it become okay for some sixteenth-century European Christians to throw off the yoke of authority of Christ's Church and follow their own ideas of what is true? Had Paul's words ceased to apply?

Now, Pastor Neil seemed to mean "church" in the smallest sense possible: the group of people who meet at someone's home, who rent space at the local school on Sundays, or maybe are lucky enough to have their own building. The "elders" of such church are presumably whoever founded it and became pastor, and perhaps those he chose to be his assistants. But without the one, apostolic, and universal Church that Christ established, following the jurisdiction of such "elders" makes little sense. No surprise, then, that so often a person who disagrees with the elders just leaves and goes to the church down the street, or founds his own church in which *he is the elder*. We see how ridiculous these scriptural verses on unity become if Christ has no visible, authoritative Church but rather thousands of little churches—with thousands of elders all claiming rightful authority.

THE PROTESTANT'S DILEMMA

If Protestantism is true, then if a Christian needs spiritual authority in his life—whether to stave off the devil, fight sin, or make a moral ruling—he has to wade through myriad differing options. Any "elder" of any church where he feels "at home" might do. But how would he know that this elder and this church were teaching the truth of God?

31

THE MISSING SAINTS

IF PROTESTANTISM IS TRUE,

Most of Christianity's saints believed in a corrupted gospel.

When I was a Protestant, I once referred to the saints as members of "the Catholic Hall of Fame." But in reading about their lives, I also wanted them on *my* team. They were heroic in their witnessing to the Faith, even to the point of torture and grisly execution. They clearly loved Jesus and were given grace to be courageous and eloquent, following the example of St. Stephen[128] and many other faithful men and women from the Apostolic Age. Yet, to my dismay, when I delved into the writings of these great Christians, I found them to have unabashedly Romish tendencies, leading me to conclude that they cannot be looked up to as true saints, no matter how holy they may have appeared.

A Saintly Paradox

When I first started reading the lives of the saints, I felt cheated: "Why haven't I been told about all these amazingly faithful people?" Their books didn't show up *anywhere* in the Christian bookstores I went to, nor very often in the secular bookstores. I had read most of the *Left Behind* series but nothing by Augustine, Thomas Aquinas, Athanasius, or Francis de Sales. Something was wrong with that.

If I were drafting baseball players as a Protestant Christian, I would want St. Augustine on my team for his great love of Scripture, the honesty of his *Confessions*, his Protestant-friendly ideas on justification and predestination, and his philosophical wisdom. He was a monumental influence on Western Christianity and in particular on the theology of John Calvin and Martin Luther. By all accounts, he's batting cleanup for me.

But then St. Augustine has to go and say things like this:

> The succession of priests keeps me [in the Church], beginning from the very seat of the Apostle Peter, to whom the Lord, after His resurrection, gave it in charge to feed His sheep, down to the present episcopate. And so, lastly, does the name itself of Catholic, which, not without reason, amid so many heresies, the Church has thus retained; so that, though all heretics wish to be called Catholics, yet when a stranger asks where the Catholic Church meets, no heretic will venture to point to his own chapel or house. Such then in number and importance are the precious ties belonging to the Christian name which keep a believer in the Catholic Church, as it is right they should.[129]

If he had stopped there, all might have been well. We can all go astray on one or two doctrines. But St. Augustine also erred on the canon of Scripture, wrongly including the seven Catholic deuterocanonical books as inspired; he erred on baptismal regeneration, purgatory, and on his acceptance of the Church's Tradition as an authority alongside the Bible. The coup de grace was the unavoidable fact that he was a *bishop* of the Church in the fourth and fifth centuries, with all the trappings that go along with that: the Mass, hearing confessions, baptizing babies, ordaining priests, and so on.

I knew Augustine could not be on my team. Neither could St. Athanasius, St. Cyprian, St. Thomas Aquinas, or St. Francis. They all believed in papist rubbish—in the awful corruptions and accretions that the Catholic Church had added over the centuries, which a *true* saint would have been able to see through.

I also knew that the Catholic usage of the word "saint" differs from what is found in the Bible. In Scripture, saints are not those Christians who have died and gone to Christ but the members of the Church still living their earthly lives. So as a Protestant, I felt good about calling myself and my Christian friends "saints," and I may have even mentally canonized my faithful grandmother, but I was loath to apply that title in a way that the Bible did not explicitly set a precedent for.

BECAUSE CATHOLICISM IS TRUE,

Catholic saints had heroic faith in Jesus Christ and lived that faith in spirit and in truth.

Those whom the Church calls saints were men and women who loved God and who accepted his love in a way that penetrated every part of them. As a questioning Protestant, I longed to love God as they did. They were the very best that Christians could be, the fulfillment of Christ's commands to love God and one another with all our hearts. They were merciful, courageous, brilliant, humble, holy. And they were as Catholic as the pope! They believed in the Real Presence of Jesus Christ in the Eucharist, the power of confession and the other sacraments, and the authority of the Church.

As a Protestant, I failed to realize that Catholic saints were impressive, not in spite of their belief in a false religion but because they believed in a true one. In fact, if we let Catholicism be true, the behavior and lives of the saints fit perfectly. They received the Holy Spirit and his gifts and power. They bore his fruits. They were strengthened against sin by reception of the Eucharist. They remained in constant friendship with God through the sacrament of Confession. They were given graces to fulfill their vocational calls in marriage, religious life, and the priesthood. They guarded and preached the fullness of Christian truth that God entrusted to the Church. They took that gospel to the ends of the earth, and Christ blessed their efforts by making those seeds take root and grow in the hearts of men from every nation. Often they watered the ground of these evangelized nations with their own blood.

In Scripture, passages from Revelation and Hebrews suggest close kinship between the saints (Christians) on earth and those in heaven offering up their prayers to God.[130] In its doctrine of the communion of saints,[131] the Catholic Church underscores the connection that all Christians share in being joined as one body in Christ—whether here on earth or in heaven. So the term "saint" applies validly to all Christians, whether alive or dead, who live in God's love and friendship.

THE PROTESTANT'S DILEMMA

If Protestantism is true, then all of the saints from the fourth century to the sixteenth believed in an adulterated gospel taught by a heretical Church. Though they may have loved God, they did so while promulgating erroneous—perhaps even evil—teachings on important matters of faith. So, although some of their piety and actions are to be commended, they cannot be looked to as Christian models to be admired and imitated. If they had only followed the Bible, they could have corrected the errors of the Church, as the later Reformers did. But sadly, for over a thousand years we have a vacuum of true Christian witness, with all the most devout and brilliant men and women hopelessly tangled up with a false gospel.

32

MARTIN LUTHER'S VIRTUE

IF PROTESTANTISM IS TRUE,

You wouldn't expect Martin Luther, the father of the Reformation, to have been an anti-Semite and polygamy supporter.

Martin Luther sparked the Protestant Reformation and formulated the key tenets still held by all Protestants today: *sola fide* and *sola scriptura*. He also had a key role in discerning the Protestant canon of Scripture. Since Protestantism's foundation is so closely tied to Luther's personal theological judgment, it's reasonable to expect that he would have had personal holiness to match.

Luther the Champion of Truth

Protestants see Martin Luther as a hero, a champion of the true faith that had been tainted by Romish errors. I recall reading one book on his life—a hagiography to be sure—that described his harrowing "escape" from the Catholics to Wartburg Castle, where he translated the New Testament into German. The popular story goes that Luther, a Catholic priest, had performed painful penances under the notion that he could win God's love and his own salvation through them. Then one day he started reading the Bible for himself, and his eyes were opened to justification by faith, rather than by works. He sought to correct the Church of her errors with a return to this biblical belief, but the Catholic authorities condemned him, causing him to flee for his life.

Of course, Protestants realize that Luther was a sinner like everyone else. But the important thing to them was that he realized he was a sinner in need of grace, unlike the Catholics who thought their paltry works could make them acceptable to God. He didn't get everything completely correct, but he got the main things right, or near enough to right to get Christianity back on track. And his own personal faithfulness was so great that even Anglicans recognize him as a saint in their calendar.[132]

BECAUSE CATHOLICISM IS TRUE,

Unsurprisingly, the architect of the Reformation was much less than a saintly man.

Catholics, who don't need to believe that Luther was a saint, can offer a much more realistic appraisal of his character. For instance, it's a fact that Luther wrote terrible things about Jewish people. In his 1543 treatise, *On the Jews and Their Lies*, Luther wrote that the Jews are "full of the devil's feces . . . which they wallow in like swine."[133] He wrote many other repugnant things about them that do not need to be repeated.

How could Luther have had God's love in his heart when he said such things of his neighbors? Certainly not many of us are completely free of all prejudice, but perhaps we should *strive* to be before we endeavor to fix God's Church. How is it possible for a man to have such a blind spot of hatred and yet also have been spiritually commissioned to reform the Church?

It might also come as a shock to Protestants that Luther, claiming *sola scriptura*, believed a Christian man could marry multiple women (polygamy):

> I confess that I cannot forbid a person to marry several wives, for it does not contradict the Scripture. If a man wishes to marry more than one wife he should be asked whether he is satisfied in his conscience that he may do so in accordance with the word of God. In such a case the civil authority has nothing to do in such a matter.[134]

A Protestant who respects Luther faces a difficult problem when confronting these facts about him, and the best solution seems to be to ignore the dark and ignorant side of his heart. Surely, on a daily basis we tolerate the flaws of our fellow men. But to Protestants Luther is not an everyday brother in Christ. He is held up as the virtuous reformer of the corrupt Church, a man so *faithful to the gospel that he alone was able to restore the true faith that had been suppressed for a millennium.*

THE PROTESTANT'S DILEMMA

If Protestantism is true, then Martin Luther, the leader of the Reformation and the primary originator of its new doctrines, should have been a saintly man, one full of love for God and neighbor; but some of Luther's writings and actions demonstrate that he was far from possessing these virtues.

33

ONGOING REFORM

IF PROTESTANTISM IS TRUE,

Nothing can stop a new "Reformation" from overturning traditional Protestant doctrines.

The Protestant Reformers disagreed on many issues. But they all seemed to agree on one thing: no Christian teaching is safe from "reform." They gutted the sacraments, modified the canon of Scripture, and defined their own theory of justification. In the 500 years that followed, their spiritual descendants have taken Reformation principles to their logical conclusion, altering or abandoning core Christian teachings—such as the divinity of Christ and inerrancy of Scripture—that the first Reformers never dreamed of questioning.

A New Reformation?

Few Protestants today agree with all the doctrines of Luther, or Calvin, or of any Reformer. Instead, it's common Protestant wisdom that you take "the good" from those guys while rejecting "the bad." And how do you know good from bad? By reading Scripture and comparing their teachings with your interpretation of it. In a sense, every Protestant since the Reformation has been a new reformer: sifting, interpreting, and assembling his own potpourri of doctrines to profess.

So Protestants are not opposed to new reformations, at least in principle. But what happens when other Protestants use *their* interpretation of Scripture to arrive at reformed doctrines that you think are fundamentally unscriptural and therefore un-Christian?

One day my wife and I drove by a church building in our town and spotted its electronic marquee proclaiming the "Bishop Spong Lecture Series." John Shelby Spong is a retired Episcopal bishop whose infamously creative heterodoxy can be discovered in his many books, in which he denies or re-invents most of the core doctrines of traditional Christianity.

Unsurprisingly, Bishop Spong sees a need for a new Reformation, and calls for it with his "twelve theses":

> Martin Luther ignited the Reformation of the six-teenth-century by nailing to the door of the church in Wittenberg in 1517 the 95 Theses that he wished to de-bate. . . . My theses are far smaller in number than were those of Martin Luther, but they are far more threatening theologically. The issues to which I now call the Christians of the world to debate are these:
>
> 1. Theism, as a way of defining God, is dead. So most theological God-talk is today meaningless. A new way to speak of God must be found.
> 2. Since God can no longer be conceived in theistic terms, it becomes nonsensical to seek to understand Jesus as the incarnation of the theistic deity. So the Christology of the ages is bankrupt.
> 3. The biblical story of the perfect and finished creation from which human beings fell into sin is pre-Darwin-ian mythology and post-Darwinian nonsense.

4. The virgin birth, understood as literal biology, makes Christ's divinity, as traditionally understood, impossible.[135]

The list continues, but I think four items will suffice to give you an idea of how radical Spong's ideas area. Nonetheless, Spong "gets" Protestantism, and has banked on its founding principle to gain acceptance for his own reformation program. He is not an isolated case but is just one representative example of the ever-reforming face of Protestant Christianity.

Not to be outdone by Spong, after the Very Rev. Gary R. Hall became Dean of the (Episcopal) National Cathedral, he announced his own unique take on Christianity: "I don't want to be loosey-goosey about it, but I describe myself as a non-theistic Christian."[136] Hall isn't sure who Jesus is: whether he really is God or just, as Hall says, "an extraordinary human being."[137] And for the head of a Protestant cathedral with national significance, God is an optional part of Christianity.

BECAUSE CATHOLICISM IS TRUE,

Doctrines of the Faith are invulnerable to substantial revision or reversal.

Bishop Spong likens himself to Martin Luther, but would traditional, Bible-believing Protestants view his "new Reformation" as a new formulation of a Christianity that has once again lost its way? More likely they would object that his theses are clearly false, because they deny the teachings of traditional Christian orthodoxy and the way that the Bible has been interpreted by the majority of Christians throughout the ages.

But why is that a problem? Luther's teachings and those

of the Reformation also denied many truths of traditional Christian orthodoxy, yet Protestants believe that his doctrinal "reforms" were correct and justified. After all, it is Protestantism that democratized the Church and made biblical interpretation accessible to all, such that an individual like Bishop Spong is not bound by any institutional church authority but is free to discover and denounce errors in what Christians have always believed, based on how he interprets the Bible.

Spong and Hall understand the Protestant reforming principle well. Whenever the Church seems like it is becoming out of touch with society or irrelevant, not even the most cherished teachings are safe from the reformer's ax.

But in the Catholic paradigm, this is not so. When the Catholic Church proclaims a teaching with its full authority, that teaching is dogmatic, rendering it unchangeable. The Trinity is the Trinity forever; Unitarians need not apply. Jesus is God and man, and the phrase "non-theistic Christian" is not just oxymoronic but downright moronic. Faithful Protestants would like to claim the same thing for their beliefs, believing them to be based on authoritative and immutable scriptures, but they cannot, because history has shown that if you give a Protestant church enough time, and it will veer off into previously unthinkable heresies.

While traditional Protestants can continue to retreat into smaller and smaller enclaves that attempt to hold fast to some subset of traditional orthodoxy, the rising water will eventually reach and overtake them. Protestantism has no safeguard against it and laid the groundwork for its own undoing in its very DNA.

THE PROTESTANT'S DILEMMA

If Protestantism is true, then there is no principled reason why Spong and Hall could not start a new Reformation that would do for the Christianity of today what Luther's Reformation did for the Church in the 1500s, since, by Protestant acclaim, rejecting traditional doctrines can be a noble thing.

34

THE CORRUPTION
OF CELIBACY

IF PROTESTANTISM IS TRUE,

**The ancient practice of celibacy
meant the Church was corrupted from
the very beginning.**

Since the Reformation, all Protestant communities have categorically rejected celibacy as a discipline for their clergy. Celibate religious brothers and sisters likewise almost entirely vanished in Protestantism. Yet consecrated celibacy was practiced in the Church from the very beginning.

Celibacy Rejected

Martin Luther rejected priestly celibacy in a reaction against the Church's distinction between clergy and laity. (The Church taught that clergy were given a special mark by God in the sacrament of holy orders.) Anglican historian Alister McGrath explains this well:

> [Luther believed that the Church] is fundamentally a gathering of believers, not a divinely ordained institution with sacred powers and authority vested exclusively in its clergy.

All believers, men and women, by virtue of their baptism, are priests. Luther noted an important corollary to this doctrine: the clergy should be free to marry, like all other Christians. This right to clerical marriage rapidly became a defining characteristic of Protestantism.[138]

Once again we see Luther's influence upon the rest of Protestantism. He interpreted the priesthood of all believers to mean that no distinction existed between clergy and laity—and so clergy should be allowed to marry. Luther encouraged monks and nuns to abandon their vows, following his own example, and he soon married a former nun.

BECAUSE CATHOLICISM IS TRUE,

Celibacy for the kingdom was and is a divinely ordained practice to which some members of Christ's Church are called.

It might seem surprising that the practices of celibacy and consecrated virginity for the sake of the kingdom could be considered reasons *in favor* of the Catholic Church. Yet it is so. The basis for Catholicism's teachings on celibacy come straight from Jesus and St. Paul. Jesus addresses the question in Matthew's Gospel:

> And Pharisees came up to him and tested him by asking, "Is it lawful to divorce one's wife for any cause?" He answered, "Have you not read that he who made them from the beginning made them male and female, and said, 'For this reason a man shall leave his father and mother and be joined to his wife, and the two shall become one flesh'? So

they are no longer two but one flesh. What therefore God has joined together, let not man put asunder."

They said to him, "Why then did Moses command one to give a certificate of divorce, and to put her away?" He said to them, "For your hardness of heart Moses allowed you to divorce your wives, but from the beginning it was not so. And I say to you: whoever divorces his wife, except for unchastity, and marries another, commits adultery." The disciples said to him, "If such is the case of a man with his wife, it is not expedient to marry." But he said to them, "Not all men can receive this saying, but only those to whom it is given. For there are eunuchs who have been so from birth, and there are eunuchs who have been made eunuchs by men, and there are eunuchs who have made themselves eunuchs for the sake of the kingdom of heaven. He who is able to receive this, let him receive it" [Matt. 19:1–12].

If this passage's meaning seems unclear to us today, we can look to what the early Christians taught about this part of Matthew 19. In the fourth century Gregory Nazianzen wrote,

Marriage is honorable; but I cannot say that it is more lofty than virginity; for virginity were no great thing if it were not better than a good thing. . . . A mother she is not, but a Bride of Christ she is. The visible beauty is not hidden, but that which is unseen is visible to God. All the glory of the king's daughter is within, clothed with golden fringes, embroidered whether by actions or by contemplation. And she who is under the yoke [of marriage], let her also in some degree be Christ's; and the virgin altogether Christ's. Let the one be not entirely chained to the world (Luke 8:14), and let the other not belong to the world at all. . . . Have you chosen the life of angels?[139]

Such passages from the writings of the Church Fathers could be reproduced many times over. Although there is no explicit scriptural command for priests to be celibate (and in the Eastern Catholic tradition, married men can be ordained), the practice of celibacy among the earliest Christians offers compelling testimony to how Christ's words were understood.

St. Paul was one such celibate, and he commends virginity for the sake of the kingdom in 1 Corinthians:

> I wish that all men were as I am. But each man has his own gift from God; one has this gift, another has that. Now to the unmarried and the widows I say: It is good for them to stay unmarried, as I am. An unmarried man is concerned about the Lord's affairs—how he can please the Lord. But a married man is concerned about the affairs of this world—how he can please his wife—and his interests are divided. An unmarried woman or virgin is concerned about the Lord's affairs: Her aim is to be devoted to the Lord in both body and spirit. But a married woman is concerned about the affairs of this world—how she can please her husband (1 Cor. 7:7–8, 32–34, NIV).

We saw earlier that Protestants' rejection of celibacy for the kingdom comes not from the Bible which commends the practice, but from following a tradition begun by Martin Luther in his reaction against some abuses of clerical power. Luther overreacted to these abuses and threw out the baby with the bathwater, and all Protestantism followed suit. It is fair to ask, however, why we should follow the tradition of Martin Luther over the words of Christ and Paul?

THE PROTESTANT'S DILEMMA

If Protestantism is true, then even though Jesus established celibacy for the kingdom, and Paul affirmed it in his own life and exhorted others to it, and the Holy Spirit made this vocation within the Church fruitful for centuries, in reality it was a corrupted practice that needed to be reformed more than 1,500 years later.

FOLLOW THE TRAIL
OF AUTHORITY

For every argument that has been made in this book, a Protestant apologist could attempt a response, perhaps more eloquent and well-presented than mine. The very existence of this debate, continuing now for almost five centuries, underscores the need for each Christian to methodically explore the arguments in order to discern, with God's help and with much prayer and humility, where the fullness of the truth resides.

Lack of centralized authority is Protestantism's Achilles's heel, and the arguments of this book strike at it. Every difference between Catholics and Protestants ultimately stems from their beliefs about the source of God-given human authority in this world. Protestants claim that a set of sixty-six ancient books is the sole infallible authority. For them, the Church is a friendly gathering of believers, all of whom effectively have authority to interpret the Bible for themselves. Catholics, on the other hand, claim that God established his Church with divine authority passed on man to man, beginning with the original apostles and continuing today through the bishops, to teach and understand the truth, which he gave to her in the deposit of faith.

Based on this authority question, this books claims that the Protestant Reformation was not justified. I now ask that my Protestant sisters and brothers seriously consider how they might defend their own justification for it. Modern-day spiritual descendants of the Reformers must explain why their schisms were not schisms, or, if they were, why these schisms are justified when no others before them were.

Every Christian seeker of truth must also be convinced on two points: first, that the fullness of the portion of universal truth that Christ has revealed to us *can* indeed be discovered. (If it were otherwise, why would God go to the trouble of revealing himself to us in the first place?) Since God desires that we know the truth, he must have made it possible for us to find it and for it to be preserved from falsehoods. Secondly, that there is no "secret knowledge" that saves us. The final judgment will be of our hearts, not our knowledge base. Therefore, any search for Christian truth should be accompanied by a level of peace as we rest in the goodness of God our Father, who loves us with an everlasting love.

Authority Is God's Intention

Part of the appeal of the Protestant idea that the Bible is the ultimate authority is the seeming simplicity of it: Any literate person can pick up the Bible and read it (once it has been translated into his language), interpret it himself, and come to know divine truth. What could be better? And having it written down protects it from being corrupted like "tradition" can be. In our modern age of widespread literacy, interpreting the Bible for ourselves, meeting at our local church with other like-minded Christians, and electing our pastor (or un-electing him if deemed necessary) seems like a great way to be a Christian. Indeed, God can work through such ways of coming to know him; he clearly has.

The problem with this conception of "the Church" and of Christianity is that it is not how God *intended* us to know him. He provided a means for *all* people to know him, even before the relatively recent age of widespread literacy and the ability to print books—a time period that still represents the minority of the Christian epoch. God played a cruel joke on humanity if he intended all Christians throughout history to be like modern Protestants and know the truths of the Faith by "reading their Bibles" (which they didn't have, since Bibles were handwritten and extremely expensive, and which they couldn't have read anyway, because most were illiterate).

God knew this reality, of course, which is why he entrusted the truth to rightful leaders of his Church, the men he poured his life into: the apostles. Those then chose worthy men to succeed them, to preserve and deepen the understanding of this truth within Christ's Church—including understanding of Sacred Scripture—by the power and protection of the Holy Spirit.

Christ has called all of us to be saints—men and women in every century, whether literate or illiterate, learned or ignorant. But he *hasn't* called us all to reinvent the Church for ourselves. He has given intellectual gifts to those he has called to be priests, bishops, and theologians so that, guided by him, they could teach the Faith to all Christians, preach to those who had not yet heard of Christ, and defend the truth from the heresies that assaulted it in every age. Are the laity *also* called to teach, preach, and defend? By all means! But to define, detract, and detour? No.

Interpretation vs. Authority

In my years of engaging in ecumenical dialogue with other Christians, one thing has become obvious: Even seemingly clear biblical passages can be challenged and interpreted differently by well-meaning Christians who view them through their particular lens.

This is the case among Catholics as well as Protestants. But since Protestants believe that the Bible is the ultimate authority, there's no arbiter to say if certain interpretation is indeed flawed. To most Protestants, their interpretation of the Bible is what the Bible says.

The truth is that the Bible can support multiple interpretive paradigms, even conflicting ones (just ask Luther, Calvin, Zwingli, and the Anabaptists). So, although I have used many Bible verses to help explain Catholic teaching, the focus of this book is not so much on those verses as on authority itself, and the consequences of following the Protestant model of authority versus the Catholic one. Rather than waste time arguing who is interpreting the Bible correctly on some specific issue, we must get to the root of this fundamental question. For although it is valuable to use Bible verses to support a point, ultimately a Christian (or anyone) accepts or rejects a belief based on how he answers the more foundational question: Who is the authority here?

Jesus himself gives us the confidence that in seeking him we will find him, who is the Truth and ultimate Authority: "Ask and it will be given to you; seek and you will find; knock and the door will be opened to you. For everyone who asks, receives; and the one who seeks, finds; and to the one who knocks, the door will be opened" (Matt. 7:7–8). May Christ bless and guide your search to find and worship him in spirit and in truth (see John 4:23), and may he unite us all as one in the fullness of the truth.

ENDNOTES

1 John Calvin: Reply to Sadoleto, Translation by Henry Beveridge in John Calvin, Tracts Relating to the Reformation, Volume 1, p. 49 (Edinburgh: Calvin Translation Society, 1844).

2 See 1 Cor. 12:12–31; Col. 1:18, 2:18–20; Eph. 1:22–23, 3:19, 4:13.

3 Vincent of Lerins, Notebooks 3:5.

4 http://www.devinrose.heroicvirtuecreations.com/blog/2009/08/28/monergism-arminianism-synergism-and-the-bible/comment-page-1/#comment-59352

5 Warren Carroll, The Founding of Christendom: A History of Christendom, Volume 1 (Front Royal: Christendom Press, 1993), chapter 17. This chapter covers the missionary journeys of the apostles during the first century, up through Peer's martyrdom in Rome.

6 Irenaeus, Against Heresies, III, 3:3.

7 Eph. 2:19–20.

8 Pope Gregory I, Papal Bull of 570.

9 Westminster Confession of Faith (WCF), ch. XXXI, 4.

10 Henry Graham, Where We Got the Bible: Our Debt to the Catholic Church (Charlotte: TAN Books & Publishers, 1994), III, 2.

11 See Gen. 17:10–14.

12 See Hosea 2:23.

13 Patriarch Flavian of Constantinople to Pope Leo, 449 AD.

14 Acts of Chalcedon, session 3.

15 Some Protestants call these marks the four attributes of the Church.

16 Martin Luther, On the Councils and the Church, Part II.

17 Eph. 4:1–6.

18 Eph. 5:25–27.

19 Catechism of the Catholic Church, 830.

20 Ignatius of Antioch, Epistle to the Smyrnaeans, 8.

21 Irenaeus, Against Heresies, IV, 26.

22 Armstrong, John H. (2010-03-04). Your Church Is Too Small: Why Unity in Christ's Mission Is Vital to the Future of the Church (Kindle Locations 867–872). Zondervan. Kindle Edition.

23 This does not mean that the Church "damned him to hell." Excommunication is a medicinal discipline intended to encourage the recipient to critically and prayerfully examine their teachings and actions so that they might return to full communion with Christ's Church. See Matt. 18:15–20 and 1 Cor. 5:1–13.

24 From Luther's German translation of the New Testament, first edition: http://www.bible-researcher.com/antilegomena.html

25 Luther's Works, vol. 35 (St. Louis: Concordia, 1963), 395-399.

26 Modern-day Protestants, thankfully, tend to engage an opposite approach, submitting their ideas to Scripture, but this is only after accepting the canon crafted by the Reformers and thus influenced by their opinions.

27 http://www.bible-researcher.com/antilegomena.html

28 The scholarly opinion on whether this Jewish council at Jamnia really existed and, if so, decided the Jewish canon has shifted over the past decades, and now most scholars reject that theory. The consensus is now that the Jews closed their canon closer to the end of the second century A.D.

29 Vander Heeren, A. (1912). Septuagint Version. In The Catholic Encyclopedia. New York: Robert Appleton Company. Retrieved September 20, 2009 from New Advent: http://www.newadvent.org/cathen/13722a.htm

30 http://www.thesacredpage.com/2006/03/loose-canons-development-of-old.html

31 http://www.usccb.org/nab/bible/sirach/intro.htm

32 He decided to follow "the judgment of the churches": http://www.ccel.org/ccel/schaff/npnf203.vi.xii.ii.xxvii.html

33 John Calvin, Institutes of the Christian Religion, I, vii.1, 2, 5, John T. McNeill, ed., trans. Ford Lewis Battles, Philadelphia: Westminster Press, pp. 75–76, 80.

34 R. C. Sproul, "Now That's a Good Question!" (Nelson, 1996), p. 81–82. (Note that some attribute this idea to John Gerstner, of whom Sproul was a student.

35 Sproul concedes this point and tries to explain how he reconciles his beliefs on the Ligonier website, which is an organization he founded to spread Reformed Protestantism's understanding of the Gospel: http://www.ligonier.org/learn/qas/we-talk-bible-being-inspired-word-god-would-men-wh/

36 Several friends of mine, Protestant and formerly Protestant (now Catholic), have expressed their confusion over Sproul's statement, as have many who've commented on ecumenical blogs. They realize how nonsensical it is, since certainty cannot rest on doubt.

37 Called the Marburg Colloquy, a meeting at Marburg Castle in Hesse, Germany in early October, 1529. The transcript of the meeting can be found here: http://divdl.library.yale.edu/dl/OneItem.aspx?qc=Ad-Hoc&q=3163

38 Modalism is the idea that the Father, Son, and Spirit are different modes of the one God. It has ancient roots in the third century with the heretic Sabellius.

39 See 1 Peter 2:5–9.

40 I first ran across the idea of sanctified common sense (or intuition) in Evangelical scholar Mark Noll's writings, notably The Scandal of the Evangelical Mind, Eerdmans, 1994.

41 See especially Heb. 13:17 and also the numerous passages where St. Paul and other apostles authoritatively teach (e.g., Acts 15) and make decisions which the other Christian faithful are expected to follow.

42 This distinction is drawn from the same epistle as those two passages: 1 John 5:16–17.

43 John Armstrong, Your Church is Too Small, Ch. 3, Zondervan, 2010.

44 McGrath, Christianity's Dangerous Idea, 69–70.

45 Keith Mathison, "Solo Scriptura: The Difference a Vowel Makes" 25–29, http://www.modernreformation.org/default.php?page=article-display&var1=ArtRead&var2=19&var3=authorbio&var4=AutRes&-var5=17

46 For a comprehensive rebuttal of Mathison's argument, see the Called to Communion article: http://www.calledtocommunion.com/2009/11/solo-scriptura-sola-scriptura-and-the-question-of-interpretive-author-ity/

47 McGrath, Christianity's Dangerous Idea, 221.

48 Matt. 16:18.

49 Jn. 14:26, 15:26.

50 See Acts 15, the Council of Jerusalem.

51 Luke 10:16, Matt. 28:18–20, Matt. 10:1.

52 Jn. 16:13.

53 McGrath, Christianity's Dangerous Idea, 177.

54 Ibid. p. 176. To support these claims, McGrath references Gustav War-neck's research in the late 1800s, which has not been rebutted.

55 Ibid., p. 177.

56 Quoted in Evangelii Nuntiandi, 14, from the "Declaration of the Synod Fathers," 4: L'Osservatore Romano (27 October 1974), p. 6.

57 Apostolicam Actuositatem, 3.

58 Westminster Confession of Faith, I.VI.

59 "I warn every one who hears the words of the prophecy of this book: if any one adds to them, God will add to him the plagues described in this book."

60 Dei Verbum, 4.

61 Mark Noll, The Scandal of the Evangelical Mind (Grand Rapids: Eerdmans, 1995), 63.

62 William Webster, The Church of Rome at the Bar of History (Carlisle, Pennsylvania: Banner of Truth, 1997), 134.

63 A very readable introduction to these earliest Fathers can be found in Rod Bennet's wonderful book Four Witnesses: The Early Church in Her Own Words, Ignatius Press, 2002.

64 See the Catechism of the Catholic Church, 2262–2267.

65 Joel R. Baseley, translator, Festival Sermons of Martin Luther (Mark V Publications, 2005), 157–158.

66 J. Sollier, "The Communion of Saints," in The Catholic Encyclopedia. (New York: Robert Appleton, 1908). Retrieved November 28, 2009 from New Advent, http://www.newadvent.org/cathen/04171a.htm.

67 Protestants should realize, however, that when Catholics kneel down before a painting or statue of a saint, they are not worshiping the saint or painting but rather simply assuming a pious posture to aid in their prayer, both directly to God and also asking the saint to pray with them to God.

68 See Matt. 5:16.

69 2 King 13:21.

70 Comm. John 3:5; CO 47: 55.

71 Comm. Titus 3:5; CO 52: 431.

72 McGrath, Christianity's Dangerous Idea, 262.

73 Martin Luther, The Large Catechism, VIII, 4, http://www.iclnet.org/pub/resources/text/wittenberg/luther/catechism/web/cat-13.html

74 For a fascinating account of how Protestant theology changed from Calvin's high view of sacraments and ecclesiology to the "born-again" conversionism of modern Evangelicalism, read this in-depth article: http://www.calledtocommunion.com/2012/03/have-you-been-born-

again-catholic-reflections-on-a-protestant-doctrine-or-how-calvins-view-of-salvation-destroyed-his-doctrine-of-the-church/

75 Justin Martyr, First Apology, 61.

76 For a comprehensive list of early Christian writings and Church Fathers who explicitly taught the doctrine of baptismal regeneration, see this article: http://www.calledtocommunion.com/2010/06/the-church-fathers-on-baptismal-regeneration/

77 The Apostolic Tradition, 21:16.

78 Letters 64:2.

79 Ibid., 64:5.

80 McGrath, Christianity's Dangerous Idea, 262.

81 Luther, The Large Catechism, XIIIA, 4, http://www.iclnet.org/pub/resources/text/wittenberg/luther/catechism/web/cat-13a.html

82 Matt. 5:48.

83 Westminster Confession of Faith, XV.4.

84 CCC 1991.

85 http://www.calledtocommunion.com/2012/11/how-the-church-won-an-interview-with-jason-stellman/#comment-39963

86 Rom. 6:19, 22.

87 1 Cor. 3:12–15.

88 Catechismus Concil. Trident., II, n. 4, ex S. August. "*De Catechizandis Rudibus.*"

89 Comm. Malachi 2:14.

90 Anglican Wedding Ceremony from 1662: http://www.pemberley.com/janeinfo/compraym.html

91 Matt. 19:8.

92 Calvin, Institutes IV, 19, 18.

93 There are some Protestant charismatic communities today that anoint with oil for healing.

94 Chrysostom, On the Priesthood, 3:6:190ff.

95 Calvin, Short Treatise on the Lord's Supper, 12.

96 Ibid., 10.

97 Ibid., 34–47.

98 Robert L. Plummer, General Editor, Journeys of Faith: Evangelicalism, Eastern Orthodoxy, Catholicism, and Anglicanism, 63–64, Zondervan, Grand Rapids, Michigan, 2012. (Emphasis in original.)

99 The most (in)famous of which is Jack Chick and his "Death Cookie" tract: http://www.chick.com/reading/tracts/0074/0074_01.asp

100 Steve Ray's Crossing the Tiber (Ignatius Press, 1997) is a solid introduction to the relevant biblical passages in both Old and New Testaments.

101 John 6:29.

102 In the prior verses he uses forms of phago/esthio, the less primal verb for eating.

103 John 6:54–58.

104 See Gen. 9:4; Lev. 17:10–13; Deut. 12:16.

105 This is a simple argument, yet in over ten years of being a Catholic and hearing Protestant responses to it, I've never heard a rebuttal or even a cogent attempt at a rebuttal to it.

106 Ignatius of Antioch, Letter to the Smyrnaeans, 6:2–7:1.

107 Ambrose, Concerning Repentance, bk. 1, ch. 2.

108 See this article on a conservative Presbyterian site: http://www.opc.org/qa.html?question_id=70 and note this Catholic rejoinder: http://www.calledtocommunion.com/2009/07/apostolicity-versus-apostolic-succession/

109 Augustine, To Generosus, Epistle 53:2.

110 Clement, Letter to the Corinthians, I, 42–44.

111 Joseph Cardinal Ratzinger, Called to Communion, 114–115.

112 http://www.elca.org/Who-We-Are/Our-Three-Expressions/Churchwide-Organization/Communication-Services/News/Releases.aspx?a=4253

113 This includes groups of Presbyterians, Baptists, Quakers, and other Protestant denominations. The United Methodists are also in the middle of an acrimonious denominational debate over same-sex "marriage," with many regional conferences approving homosexual behavior and lobbying for the reversal of the current Methodist statement against it. Several Methodist pastors, including high profile ones, have already begun performing same-sex "marriage" ceremonies: http://www.kansascity.com/2013/09/27/4512746/united-methodist-high-court-to.html

114 Beginning with the Anglican denomination's acceptance of contraception within marriage at the 1930 Lambeth Conference: http://www.lambethconference.org/resolutions/1930/1930-15.cfm

115 http://www.relevantmagazine.com/digital-issue/53?page=66

116 http://www.christianitytoday.com/ct/2012/aprilweb-only/churches-contraception.html

117 http://marshill.com/2008/01/06/christian-birth-control-options

118 1 Cor. 6:9–10.

119 See Blessed John Paul II's landmark work on the Theology of the Body.

120 Pope Paul VI, Humanae Vitae, 9: http://www.vatican.va/holy_father/paul_vi/encyclicals/documents/hf_p-vi_enc_25071968_humanae-vitae_en.html

121 http://www.nrlc.org/news/1999/NRL199/sween.html Specifically, in cases where the physical or mental health of the mother was seriously threatened, or when the child would be born with a disability, or when the child was conceived in rape.

122 Though thankfully, from 1980 forward the Southern Baptist Convention changed back to a much more pro-life position.

123 http://www.thechristianleftblog.org/1/post/2012/10/the-bible-tells-us-when-a-fetus-becomes-a-living-being.html

124 Catholic Church law recognizes two exceptions, both involving marriages wherein one or both spouses aren't baptized: The Pauline Privilege, in which one non-baptized spouse decides to seek baptism but the other does not (drawn from 1 Corinthians 7:10–15), and the similar but even rarer Petrine Privilege, wherein a (non-sacramental) marriage between one baptized and one non-baptized person may be dissolved by the pope in order that one of the spouses may enter a sacramental marriage with someone else.

125 Michael Spencer, "The Original Coming Collapse Posts," Internet Monk (March 10, 2009), http://www.internetmonk.com/archive/the-original-coming-evangelical-collapse-posts.

126 McGrath, Christianity's Dangerous Idea, 219.

127 Luke 10:16, 1 Tim. 3:15, John 16:13, Matt. 16:18.

128 Acts 7.

129 Against the Fundamental Epistle of Manichaeus, 4.

130 Rev. 5:8, Heb. 12:1.

131 Catechism of the Catholic Church, 2683.

132 http://en.wikipedia.org/wiki/Calendar_of_saints_%28Episcopal_Church_in_the_United_States_of_America%29

133 Obermann, Heiko. Luthers Werke. Erlangen 1854, 32:282, 298, in Grisar, Hartmann, Luther. St. Louis 1915, 4:286 and 5:406, cited in Michael, Robert. Holy Hatred: Christianity, Antisemitism, and the Holocaust. New York: Palgrave Macmillan, 2006, p. 113.

134 Martin Luther, De Wette, II, 459.

135 http://en.wikipedia.org/wiki/A_New_Christianity_for_a_New_World.

136 http://www.washingtonpost.com/lifestyle/style/from-comedy-to-national-cathedral/2013/08/01/683906e2-f884-11e2-8e84-c56731a202fb_story_1.html

137 Ibid.

138 Alister McGrath, Christianity's Dangerous Idea: The Protestant Revolution—A History from the Sixteenth Century to the Twenty-First (New York: HarperOne, 2007), 52.

139 Translated by Charles Gordon Browne and James Edward Swallow. From Nicene and Post-Nicene Fathers, Second Series, vol. 7. Edited by Philip Schaff and Henry Wace. (Buffalo, NY: Christian Literature Publishing Co., 1894.) Revised and edited for New Advent by Kevin Knight. http://www.newadvent.org/fathers/310237.htm